GROUNDSWELL

ISBN: 978-1-7344984-3-1

Cover image: Nina Berfelde
Cover design: Travis Sharp
Book design: Blair Johnson

Essay Press is a non-profit 501(c)(3) organization dedicated to publishing innovative, explorative, and culturally relevant prose.

www.essaypress.org

Distributed by Small Press Distribution
1341 Seventh Street
Berkeley California 94710
spdbooks.org

GROUNDSWELL

Yanara Friedland

ON DE-MATRICULATING: BORDER WORK 2.0 IN *GROUNDSWELL*

Jill Magi

There are two "de-matriculations" within *Groundswell* that I want to highlight by way of an introduction—two instances where, as Yanara Friedland articulates, there is registration and belonging, yet "[s]everance is the great locutor."

"Matriculate" comes from the Latin "matricula" or register, which is a version of the Latin "matrix," the ground or environment in which something is held, lodged, housed. In printmaking, matrix is also the term used for the ground prepared in order to make an image.

First, there is the story of pulled wisdom teeth—a minor surgery on one side of the jaw where the extraction took place in the States, and on the other side of the jaw, these remaining teeth are pulled "back" in Berlin, her city of birth. Friedland looks at her teeth in the dentist's tray. Her gums swell. Language's sounds must adjust. The jaw bone, a matrix that once held these entities, remains as a permeable matrix: "The teeth will be thrown away. The city will stay in my bones."

Friedland has "returned" to this place in order, in part, to be a guest scholar in a linguistics course at the University Viadrina in Frankfurt Oder, a border town to Poland a train ride away. This is a familiar story of matriculation: placing oneself around a seminar table, receiving the curriculum, permitting some kind of susceptibility via learning. An embeddedness in a university, that enlightenment place of promise: our most common use of the word "matriculate." Yet this registration will not hold her. While the talk in the seminar is of patterns and deviations, she chooses non-alignment and de-matriculates. Yet the linguistics professor is not unsympathetic to Friedland's remove. Outside of class, approaching the bridge that crosses the River Oder, the professor reassures her, "you will find something here. For women the spaces begin to open."

Indeed, the alternate project, located below ground, reveals itself. In the basement of an affiliated university in the same town, she finds the seminar's double: an archive of German-Polish border stories. I love basements and any siting of them in literature! Or: the work of literature as a basement. In New England, the loamy and often dark place where I live when I don't live in the clear and dry desert of Abu Dhabi, one sometimes finds basement graves inside old houses! Where could one find a better space for the body of the beloved? Basements: the lung-space of a building, an institution, a domicile. Holding emptiness, what is stored there may be both susceptible to mold and protected from degrading light. Basement: where meaning may require mediation and is not yet completely disciplined, or where meaning is deposited as if moved into de-matriculated status. Friedland calls the stories she finds there "star maps" for their partiality—for the intense old light rocketing out of the darkness of distance. Refusing traditional matriculated status, Friedland here recovers stories, translates them, and brings them into new ground which is the matrix that is *Groundswell*. There is a beautiful and generous section of the book where each section holds the first name of the friend Friedland has, in this basement, made. Friedland's first person narrative extends to these subjects and there is an intimacy I cherish in those particular pages.

The final de-matriculation episode: it is on the occasion of her semester-ending presentation as guest scholar when Friedland experiences her de-matriculated status as complete. She calls it a failed presentation. This tips me off to the poetry of what she has presented, and indeed it is the seed of the book *Groundswell*. Many of us are familiar with being the poet at the conference and the confusion that what I think of as our "uncategorizable precision" solicits. And so this scene unfolds in a familiar way. No one asks questions. Then a professor decides to comment, questioning her methodology. In the midst of this, fellowship comes to the rescue! Friedland's friend Nina pulls her away. She waves as she exits. A picnic and a swim await the two friends.

This reminds me of another story of an exit: a poet in need of a full-time job is asked to be a visiting writer for a year. It doesn't really pay the bills, but the poet agrees to the position, hoping for something more permanent but that doesn't come through. At a public year-end celebration for all the newly-graduated MFAs, the poet is asked to come to the stage where she is presented with a hard-cover copy of a biography of a famous poet as a thank you, a parting gift. She is a mix of baffled, speechless, humored, slightly insulted, and ultimately left wanting. During the tentative applause, she exits the stage, but she doesn't turn away from the presenter; rather, clutching the book and smiling, she moonwalks toward the stairs! This is not planned. Exhaustion makes new moves—for a moment she publicly glides, forging a silky texture above the rocky ground of contingent labor.

*

I once made a studio discovery that was hardly a discovery: it was right there all along. Painting, I found that borders are charged, important spaces—how one color will meet the other matters. How difficult it is to make a border by actual edge meeting edge—usually a border is executed by placing one brushstroke atop a territory that already exists. Or it is made through blending, so that the border eases into territory, sometimes only suggesting that one plane has ended and another has begun. Borders are sometimes the image-space that makes all the difference in how the painting is read. In Chinese painting traditions, image is placed upon a ground so that the image or text seems to float. Here, I think that borders are not so charged. Within the western art context, it may be a marker of the post-modern to not fill things in perfectly, to leave a halo of white space around contour lines, revising the western fresco's compulsion to correct the giornata. It is as if we have grown weary of the sheen of complete territories meeting neat borders.

Speaking of weariness, prior to reading *Groundswell* I wondered if everything had been said, already, about borders. I am suspicious of the empathetic representation of the refugee and migrant and I thought that maybe borders—used as metaphor, particularly—had become commodified, almost pornographic, a kind of stance that worked very well to generate pity and to keep meditations on complicity at bay.

But what is found in *Groundswell* is not an explication of the problem of borders, but the articulation of conjunctions: territories always touch borders. And the territories made in relation to the border are themselves negotiated, relational; territories stand always in relation to the border, a place where it is not possible to stay. Into this situation, what is agency? How can a book lead us into real border space—show us its rooms, features, its dimensions, its textures? Reading *Groundswell*, I never got the feeling that Friedland is out to make a claim about justice or the futility of borders and their walls. No tone of indictment. And so, *Groundswell* is "border work 2.0" whose primary mode and analytic I would say, is exhaustion.

What if there is no possibility of removing the border? What if history has not progressed into betterment so that countries still talk about building walls, and in fact new walls are being built? Where has the victory of the coming down of the Berlin wall lead us? Nowhere.

So, into exhaustion we go. In its work with no solution, no epiphany, no landing on one side or the other, no progress, I felt a promise within the pages of *Groundswell*. Exhaustion as method. Exhaustion as nothing to fear, and taken for what it is, perhaps exhaustion contains within it some vitality we may be unpracticed at recognizing. We certainly do not design it—and therein lies the key. Exhaustion's vitality cares little about betterment or pre-determined outcome—it is a kind of "giving up" in order to give everything to something brand new—

"When ground swells all eyes go under."

If seeing is knowing, then *Groundswell* asks for another sense. If the amphibious existence is what is required, *Groundswell* proposes a way. Maybe black studies can also help us imagine such a tradition and metaphysical situation. In *Black and Blur*, the first book of his trilogy on black art and ontology, Fred Moten queries into the persistence of anti-blackness and the utterances that emerge within the context of a lack of redress: "Is a problem that can't be solved still a problem?" He queries further: if an individual will never overcome anti-blackness, or be restored by a system that actually creates "freedom" right alongside anti-blackness, then this fact displaces the possibility of the singularity of the individual, of traditional notions of individual agency. Instead of some kind of individualized therapeutic possibility, Moten further claims, the situation is exhaustion: felt and experienced but not because of one's singular blackness. What emerges is ". . . a certain apposition conceived of not as therapy but alternative operation." I think it is an operation, exhausted, with almost nothing to lose—no fear, even if terror is a constant companion.

The border, in its reality, is one of the most obviously psychotic, inauthentic, contested and yet vigilantly patrolled realities that reminds us we are not ever in possession of individuation, freedom, autonomy, sovereignty. The questioning of national boundaries extends, for Friedland, to the questioning of a bounded and bordered individual. She writes: "This land, where trains depart by the hour and the forest is muddy history, a rotten bagpipe. Everything is fear, and here, rightness." I read Moten, and Yanara Friedland's *Groundswell,* as a warning against the too-muscular liberal subject who believes in the "rightness" of, for example, the German state capable of endowing each citizen with belonging or not. Friedland's sensing language reminds us that though The Wall came down, the nation, with real estate and rampant capitalism creating more invisible borders, has little or maybe nothing to be proud of.

Another apposite story comes to mind. In her 2018 explanation of why it is that she will not protest or contest the banning of her book in her home country of Kuwait, Mai Al Nakib claims exhaustion: "My exhaustion derives from a sense that both the problem and the solutions it solicits have remained relatively static for at least two millennia."

She continues, "Writing through repressive bans and the din of protest alike—in other words, sidestepping both the for and against—in the name of a future unguaranteed, but no less important for that, is to me the pressing concern."

Yanara Friedland's book makes a future that unfolds despite the existing matrix, or in excess of it—this making is a movement that must dislodge, must mis-use, must de-matriculate in order for a new registration, a new alignment. *Groundswell* connects to the beautiful traditions of things not quite aligning as expected, the overlaps and gaps emitting a beautiful howl where the making is laid bare in perfect failure. Quoting from Martin Shaw's "A Culture of Wildness," *Groundswell* ends with the humming claim that " 'underneath the concrete and underneath the towns an old ancient dreaming spirit is waiting for people to live in the right way, and when you do it you have a kind of genius underneath you that you as a person don't just possess.' " Friedland replies: "There is a mound that I address. A stone from your body, a comma separating your name, your longing organ, your loudest dog, broken languages rising."

*

As this is an introduction, a kind of future index, and because I fear foreclosing discovery in this prose, I want, finally, to tantalize future readers with a representation of the combinatory matrix—the stunning appositions, not comparisons or contrasts—that is *Groundswell*:

There is Hannah Arendt, a conference, a pilgrimage, a border, another border, a jaw, teeth, a seminar, a professor, a middle school class near the border with Mexico, a monastery, a desert, a river, Berlin, Tucson, another border, a swim, a picnic, a presentation, an archive, a cat and its death and the appearance of a visitor-cat. Monsoon, the city built on a swamp, the university basement, a bridge, a Jewish cemetery, a museum. Thomas Brasch, Ghayath Almadhoun, Saskia Sassen, Walter Benjamin, Home Office officials, an Iranian man seeking asylum, an exhibition in Marseille, the Tiergarten, Mariam Ghani, a train station, the Verboten/Forbidden exhibit, the Organ Pipe Cactus National Monument, a border patrol guard, a priest, the Canadian border, London, an apartment, a garden, another apartment, another garden, sand, water, prison economies, real estate economies, walls commodified and as commodities, borders, territories, languages, and dreams.

We used to invent all kinds of stories about the Border. In the evenings we scared each other by speculating what would happen if we crossed. . . . We, as children, did not know the meaning of the Border, but we sensed from our parent's talk that it was something terrible, something that kills you if you get too close to it.

(Enni from Parikkala)

The meditation needs to be simple. Think of a landscape, a lake, a field, maybe a river. You move away from your holding. It might be aridity or the walls of a room. When you leave, take an item with you, one that catches your attention. You walk where you see the path, unless something calls for you to traverse waves, a desert, a line. Notice what you meet, who appears. At every gate there are guardians. At every threshold there are questions. As you approach the limit, the seductive rim, or a line drawn by hand into the sand, remember: There is no return. There is multiplication. The burying of the body in many places.

GRENZE · CHOROGRAPHY
HINTERHAUS · FORMATION
PARALLEL TIME · DEPARTURE
UNIVERSITY · TWIN CITY
WHITE ZONES · HUMAN DESTINIES
WAR · RIVER · GDR
NOTEBOOK · LANDFLUCHT
POST-TRANSGRESSION SYNDROME
PILGRIMAGE · OYNEG SHABBES
CEMETERY · ORACLE ROAD
STATELESS · DIGLOSSIA · AUGURY
MOONSCAPES · TRAINSTATION
GROUNDSWELL · CROSSINGS

GRENZE

I come from the border, *Grenze, Grenzstreifen,* nation, wall, barbed wire, west that is east that is a city and also a consciousness of rivers. I come from the swell, a city built on swamp. Whatever ground it is that grew me, the lines run firmly through it. The gray mother spat, sank into the zones, with hard bones in the hold. Mostly dependent on the other side, placing stone onto stone onto stone. The uneven shapes that allow for holes.

Distances keep secrets. That is to say, a map can also be departure, deviance, decline. Its variant narratives both durable and permeable.

I want the inner cartography and the legend to expose a weave, a map both coming from far away and from deep within.

Asking: what if the border itself began to talk, to oracle, to direct?

CHOROGRAPHY

In the sixteenth century, Sebastian Münster wrote his *Cosmographia*, interviewing scholars, seafarers, locals, cartographers, and writers about the world and everything in it. The Americas, forty years before their "official discovery," are only peripherally imagined. The pyramids of Egypt described as quite small. Frankfurt Oder is shown with its river and some rowboats, in the background the church and a conglomeration of houses. It is considered the first cartographic representation of the town. The woodcut positions the artist on the other side of the river (now Poland), and shows its bridge and bustle from a distance. This side, the observing one, a continuation of fields and woods, is not part of the woodcut. Münster's *Cosmographia* attempted to map through local descriptions, anecdotes, and observation and became, next to the Bible, one of the most read books in Germany at the time.

HINTERHAUS

Berlin is rainy and overcast. Summer delayed by a weather event named Elvira. The year 2016. Precarious times. In a small room in a Hinterhaus apartment the dead poet appears in my dreams. I know she is dead but here, fully alive, exhilarating and thin. The dead poet talks of happiness, which, she says, is not found in ridiculous salaries. Then walks up to a dark stage to read. The technician has disappeared. The lights are out. The dog is half cat. Afterwards, we exit together, and I thank her many times.

The German word Hinterhaus refers to Berlin's courtyard architecture, where some apartments are only accessible once you cross through the courtyard to the "back house," the house within the house. The room is just big enough for a mattress from where I can see the chestnut tree. Occasionally voices travel along the walls.

Within the rooms of the imagination sits a clavis, a device that can name and insurrect affinities. It absorbs words, intimacies, and sometimes the taste of a good ingredient for its task. And the task is to reflect, like mercurial waters, what is given what is found, what is understood what is still unknown. Inside a body there are also hallways. The clavicle is a bone, a strut connecting shoulder blade and sternum. Now bludgeon those words; smash them together into a cool space.

FORMATION

We lived on Nollendorfstrasse. Close to Nollendorfplatz. Hinterhaus with views onto a square-shaped courtyard with a little sandbox, some trees, and a defunct elevator. I remember faces and shopping bags and sounds. The various characters that lived there (and I say characters because the whole episode displays itself now like a scene from a play) had children, cats, croaky throats, secrets, watermelons in netted bags. My first vocation was the study of people, staring at them, and my apprenticeship began in this courtyard. Rough-looking pigeons nested in the defunct elevator. I was perpetually dirty, running around barefoot, and in summer racing between Nollendorfplatz and the house, carrying an armful of ice cream cones back to a rotating group of adults who lingered by the sandbox. Nollendorfplatz was then a prominent junkie hangout littered with needles. Some drunks yelled belligerently at people in line for ice cream. The people in line tried their best to ignore their presence, studying the various flavors. The unspoken instruction was to pretend they didn't exist. I wondered if looking directly at them would draw them closer. Something I felt ambivalent about. So, I too began to study the flavors, though I knew even before leaving the house that I wanted chocolate and raspberry. Raspberry first and chocolate on top. Above us lived a woman who had a bulldog and worked as a prostitute. For my birthday she bought me a plastic fish, which remained one of my favorite toys throughout childhood. I often played with some boys a few years older than me, who kindly took me along on their adventures to Winterfeldtplatz. We practiced roller skating and built a skateboard ramp. Occasionally we hung onto the backs of garbage trucks and let ourselves be pulled across the square. One of the boys was learning to play the piano. He lived in an apartment diagonal from ours, and during summer evenings we both opened our windows while he played Beethoven's Ninth Symphony for me. Across from our apartment lived an Italian family. Everyone in the courtyard knew he was mafia and that he beat up his wife. She would throw herself half out the window and yell, "he is killing me" or "I am bleeding." A few times the police came, and the next day everything would be quiet. Afterwards she usually went out, shopping with her little boy, a tyrant of four, who had attacked me several times in the courtyard. When she arrived with her shopping bags, she called her husband's name and his face appeared promptly, opening the window and carefully descending a wicker basket past windows along the house wall. She put her groceries into the basket and he pulled firmly at the string to which it was attached. The groceries dangled past windows and sometimes threatened to tip over. His wife looked anxiously at the ascending basket, while her tyrant boy threw stones against the facade. Several years later her husband went to prison. The courtyard rumor suggested that he had murdered someone. What no one anticipated, however, was that her son would take exceptional care of his heartbroken mother, turning into an all-around gentle and soulful man. The courtyard was covered in shit. For years a petition advocated for the eviction of one of the few people who owned an apartment in the building, a fairly rare circumstance in Berlin in the '80s. This landlord was the personification of the evils of capitalism. He was the only person who had a roof terrace, a built-in kitchen, and he let his large dog shit everywhere. A fact that was frequently discussed among the renters, alongside possible strategies to hold the capitalist accountable. I never met this man in person; he dwelled higher up, in his airy open-floor-plan penthouse. He symbolized the threat of real estate hawks buying up run-down buildings to refurbish and sell them for high prices to investors. When I returned to the Nollendorfstrasse in my early twenties, this had become very much a reality. All the original renters were gone, and when I rang the doorbell to our old apartment a well-known filmmaker opened. Our apartment, he proudly showed me, had been transformed into guest quarters connected to another much larger apartment with chandeliers and gleaming wood floors. He asked me if we were the family that produced the peeled off wallpaper in the hallway. I responded proudly, yes, we were that family, but the act was wholly my responsibility. Besides peeling off wallpaper during my early childhood, I had also been preoccupied with kitten adoptions. I always hoped to run into the two women who lived on the west side of the building. They had told me about the difference between spring kittens and fall kittens. The ones born in fall were much cozier and less active than the spring ones, they explained. With these women I imagined possible kitten adoption scenarios, the pros and cons of taking care of a spring kitten versus a fall kitten. In the end I got no kitten at all. There was constant gossip coursing through the hallways of the Nollendorfstrasse 28, and I, too, began to spread stories. In one instance I had decided that a very shy and bookish woman who lived in a ground floor apartment was a witch. She was, in fact, a writer. For weeks I told my friends that this witch was very powerful, and we peeked around corners of the courtyard in an imagined game of spying and hiding from her spells. When she suddenly appeared in the staircase, loaded with books and very absent-mindedly walked passed me, I shivered with ecstasy. The confrontation was real and I had survived it. Another writer, who I only saw once coming through the breezeway, had written a book called *Krankheit als Weg*. Both my parents frequently referenced this book. Illnesses and their psychological root causes were explored in detail, and while I liked getting lost in entries, I am certain that its reading influenced my rather psychosomatic orientation towards illness, with a compulsive tendency to interpret symptoms alongside possible psychological disturbances. The staircases were old and musty. My brother and I often slid down the wooden railings and scared Potjo, the black cat, cooling off on the steps. On certain long summer nights everyone was at their windows and conversed across the open space, watering flowers or discussing the news of the day. Our apartment was on the first floor and mostly run-down, which allowed for the rent of 400 Deutschmark to never be raised as long as we lived there. When the wall came down, this Hinterhaus community began to crumble, people moved, some bought cheaper apartments in the east or fled elsewhere from the real estate takeover. The enclosure of courtyards, the way they render the sky square shaped, remains emblematic not only of Berlin but also of my childhood. These scenes have since blended in my mind with the rare color footage of Berliners of earlier times, observing armed forces cart in stones, mortar, and barbed wire. People by their windows staring in disbelief, almost motionless, at the rising wall, while others simply flung themselves beyond their sills.

PARALLEL TIME

"The Age of Genius," one of the fragments that survive from Bruno Schulz's vanished book *Messiah*, evokes the necessity for parallel streams of time. A little problematic, to be sure, he admits, "but when one is burdened with contraband of supernumerary events that cannot be registered, one cannot be too fussy."

Schulz was shot by a Gestapo officer while walking home with a loaf of bread. He had been granted protection by another Gestapo officer in the Drohobycz Ghetto in exchange for a mural of fairytales painted at the officer's residence for his children.

In the lost manuscript, *Messiah,* childhood is understood as the primary mystic and messianic time. The artist, so Schulz believed, only has a handful of images to work from, which all originate from these first experiences. "It is my longing," he wrote, "to mature toward childhood."

DEPARTURE

I was gifted my long-awaited cat several decades later, after I moved to the US. The cat had survived despite her humble beginnings in an abandoned garage in the mountains of Colorado. A friend found her as a kitten. It seemed she had lived in the garage for several months, hunting mice, spiders, and ghosts. Sleeping in a toolbox. After we adopted her she endured large snowstorms, our move to the desert, the impenetrable heat of southern Arizona, and a long absence from us, passed with several caretakers.

When we departed the mountains and moved to the desert, and after the car broke down in Truth or Consequences, the gradual shift from arid mountain plateaus to a blooming green landscape left us speechless. We expected heat but instead the monsoon rains carried our moving truck along the empty streets of Tucson. Did anyone live here? Was this some afterlife? The cat sat on my lap, licking my hand.

Out of the constraint came an impulse. Out of the impulse an idea. Out of the idea a thought. Out of the thought a limitation. Out of the limitation a sand. Out of the sand a periphery. Out of the periphery a distance. Out of the distance a horizon. Out of the horizon a dirt. Out of the dirt a trace. Out of the trace a continuation. Out of the continuation a despair. Out of the despair a hypothesis. Out of the hypothesis a gestation. Out of the gestation a reproduction. Out of the reproduction a pathology. Out of the pathology a miracle. Out of the miracle a failure. Out of the failure an expulsion.

On some evenings, when we couldn't find the cat in the maze of our desert garden, I spoke to her anxiously in my head, *come home now, come back, it's getting late.* And she usually heard me, appearing suddenly from some dark corner or the wooden panels of the compost. Her body's appearance, the stretch of her front legs and white shiny paws, indicated safety and rest. The body close and heaving. At night I can still sometimes see her coming out of the deepest recesses of a corner or balancing along a wall.

I remember it rained, a Sunday, the second consecutive day of rain, a marker for the bloom about to unleash. Eventually the cat went outside. In no remarkable manner except, and this might be the only moment that indicated another reality unfolding alongside the familiar drum of the day, that she walked over the stone patio to the water bowl below the tree. I remember her walking and thinking that there was something pitiful or miserable in her posture. I put it down to the rain and her sleepy demeanor. Her fur quality reappeared in my dream last night, slightly furrowed, the way it had been that day as she bent down to drink. In place of the water bowl there is now a candle, a piece of bark marking her existence. In my dream last night, she appeared for the first time very lethargic and on the verge of dying. We prepared a fluid food for her, which took hours, and I lost my temper. Finally it was ready. She devoured it and immediately started to feel better.

How is hunger or our lack thereof an indicator of our misgivings? I barely ate for two weeks, but now with this new foundational emptiness taking root everywhere, I can't stop myself from eating; a perpetual but groundless appetite. Thought patterns start to become protracted as well, partly absent, as if locked up, partly reoccurring and obsessive, also as if locked up. One of the reoccurring ones: I will only be able to return home if I am either famous, old, or under circumstances unnamable. There is no exact reasoning behind this thought. It lifts up and lands haphazardly somewhere in the peripheries.

That Sunday we went for a walk at Gates Pass part of the Tucson Mountains. Before we left, neither of us thought about looking for the cat. Many times she had been invisible during the day, seeking her own throughways, secret dwellings and relationships. The garden in its unkemptness ideal for her variegated pursuits. In the back, by the salt cedar, a bone yard of her tormented dead victims half buried. Below the mesquite she observed mourning doves that moved obliviously. On the neighbor's porch she would sit at sunset and watch the street. The moldy trunk of a cactus in the front yard where she greeted us as we came home. The large bush, where she rested and waited and from where she cried out three times before dying. But there are other places, places unknown to us. I imagine she lived alongside creatures, with birds and lizards, exchanging intimacies.

After our walk, the entire desert bathed in a smell of creosote and water and already dark, we stopped by the grocery store to pick up some food. Everything is biography and sentence. Everything returns with the taste of foreboding. The gate made a particular sound. As soon as we entered, we heard her scream desperate and loud, massive, like a beacon. We called her name, and she screamed again. It was coming from a bush, another one whose name I don't know, large and with silvery green leaves. And she screamed again. We couldn't see well, wrestled a flashlight from somewhere. I already knew then, gasped, and searched for my phone while Robert dove into the shrubbery. I heard his cry, "what happened, oh, no, what happened." He carried her towards me, and I expected a mauled body. Instead she lay limp in his arms, her eyes massive and black and dilated, the way I had seen them once in a rabbit, also dying, and which had always reminded me of two distant planets. There were no wounds or blood on her body. Later, the vet listed the million possible causes that would remain unanswered. Poison from one of the sprawling yards, liver failure, a sick mouse close to our neighbor's chicken coop, a spider's bite from the undertunnels. Threats from below, across, and beyond our little garden, or from deep within. She was perfectly intact. We laid her down on a pillow and watched over her body for the rest of the night. Then buried her, rolled into a large blanket I had brought back from the Himalayas several years ago. Her scream, we both believe, was her last act, a gesture of love allowing us to find her.

After that Sunday the garden began to dry out. A wilting mood in the branches pervaded the mornings. The grave of our cat now decorated with seashells from a recent trip to Mexico. I spent most days at my desk. My back bent weighed down by a large wall of rosebushes. At times I could not distinguish myself from the plants outside of the house. Their health or dryness somehow also a symptom that grew in my own body. Cats of all colors began to move through the desert-landscaped garden, evidence that the gatekeeper was fully gone, below the earth. One cat, black with some brown dots, I initially mistook for our dead one. Some underworld version of her with parts of her left ear missing and her tail thin and corroded, barely attached. She looked so emaciated that I put a bowl of some leftover cat food outside of our door. I did not see her eat but simply filled the empty bowl each morning.

Several weeks later I sat outside writing. The black cat with brown spots deliriously crossed the stone patio. Delirious, because she did not really walk but sway, her tail almost gone. At one point she stopped, turned around, and in her narrow face the look of bleak defeat. I brought out the bowl, far enough away from the table, and watched her devour the dry food. I could not decide what she looked like: downtrodden or ill, abandoned or glorious. I could not tell whether she was a kitten or a starved grandmother. I called her Yogila. It seemed she had died several times but somehow, whether by mistake, good fortune, or curse, returned here. Fragmented and alive. The feeding ritual continued and she stopped by daily, always weary, her eyes both on the plate and on me. I stared at her without restraint. The sediments began to swirl. A ground of convulsions, of some story. I continued to be the woman with a notebook who passes through. At night, when it was not cool but cooling everything began to travel, while above the helicopters swarmed the sky in widening circles.

UNIVERSITY

I leave the desert in the summer of 2016 to live in Berlin for the first time since my family's departure more than twenty years ago. It is a temporary living, enabled by Viadrina University, some one hundred miles east of Berlin, where I am welcomed as a researcher of uncertain discipline. Four times a week I take the train out east to Frankfurt Oder. It was from its city limits that the Red Army moved into full offensive to occupy Berlin. The Germans burned down the bridge, which connected the two parts of the city and below which the river Oder flows. The Potsdam Agreement divided Frankfurt Oder, one side belonging to Germany and the other to Poland. The line was not drawn but asserted with the narrow side of a hand. Frankfurt Oder, the German side, retained its original name and became part of the GDR post-World War II. Its other half was named Slubice. A handball team traveled between the two cities.

I descend the steep hill from the train station towards the university. The street I must cross is called Priester Strasse. What are the priests doing so close to the university? Once I have crossed, I become a visiting researcher of the linguistics seminar. Already I have trespassed; try to become a linguist within an hour. But the trespass is more an assimilation, a reflex that has enabled me to move into foreign spaces without drawing too much attention. The professor says things like "language is a local practice" or "there is no 'pure' data" and "no observation survives without theory." I have a desire to out myself, declare insanity or at least misunderstanding. I am not a scholar, especially not a linguistics scholar. Somehow I fooled entire clusters to affect what? The professor reminds the class that innovation can only function if it incorporates existing patterns, and if the recipients respond positively to the innovation. She illustrates this through an example of puppets, improv music, and writing. "Of course, you can always act against patterns," she adds. "You could rip the piece of paper apart and burn it, rather than read and understand it." Again I consider fleeing. But the question remains: from what?

TWIN CITY

Frankfurt Oder and its Polish twin city, Slubice, lie at the periphery of their countries and are often perceived to be nowhere. The river Oder, the second largest in Poland, passes Wroclaw, snails along Germany's edges before emptying into the Baltic Sea. A place that was divided and stuck back together innumerable times. After World War II an entire population exchange took place. People from eastern Poland—areas that are now part of Lithuania, Belarus, and Ukraine—repopulated the Polish side, which was German before the war. Germans were expelled. During the 1950s attempts to justify Slubice's Polish roots led to tracing the area back to 1000 BC, inhabited then by the Piasts, one of the first ruling dynasties of Poland. A ministry for renaming emerged, and German street names became Polish. Nowadays people cross to one side to buy high quality washing powder, to the other to purchase cheap cigarettes, alcohol, asparagus. Some claim their relationship, cooperation and coexistence a success story. "We share everything, even heating. Our children learn both languages and there is a bus line between the two towns. We exchange our jobs occasionally. Right now the mayors have swapped offices." Others say that the Poles are working hard to integrate into German learning systems, whereas Germans rarely learn Polish. Some believe Slubice would love to belong more fully to Germany, but Germans keep a friendly distance and drop off their old clothing at the gates. After dark some won't cross the bridge anymore.

WHITE ZONES

Shortly after my arrival in Berlin, on a sunny afternoon, I have my remaining wisdom teeth removed. The teeth lie large and bloody on a tray. The right side was taken out before I left the continent. The left side is now gone, too, as I practice my return. Once the teeth are gone, their memory remains in the pink flesh of the scar. For the first time in decades I feel a contraction in my body. I am unable to concentrate. I can smell the faint smoke of cigarettes from a neighboring apartment. There is also a choked sensation, a field at the center of planetary motion. This area is storage to a million different feelings, comingling and feasting on the field. I have not been here in so many years, distracted myself with plans, travels, conversations in avoidance of this, how to call it, incomparable ruin.

On the train, heading east to Frankfurt Oder, I read poems by the Polish poet Jerzy Ficowski who wrote: "When something disappears in the world an empty space is created. When I enter this space, I can begin to perceive what once happened here. Warsaw's ghetto, now Muranow, did not even have ruins." In Ficowski's poem sequence "Errata," which means printing error, the poem becomes the smuggled unofficial version of history that cannot be otherwise transported.

A white zone is an area that is no longer publicly accessible. Removed from all maps, it is left to itself or reimagined for highly specialized purposes. For example, after a bark beetle invasion the Soviet army occupied a piece of land along the Polish-German border. During the 1950s it became a shooting range for tanks and infantry. After 1989 the Soviet army retreated and Germany developed plans to make it the biggest bomb target practice area in Central Europe. The 140 kilometers of thick forests were declared "a military white zone" and became a prohibited area after local residents formed a large citizens' initiative "to free the landscape."

The teeth will be thrown away. The city will stay in my bones.

HUMAN DESTINIES

I had watched the collapse of the wall sitting on my father's shoulders, eating a man made of dough who was smoking from a clay pipe. After I ate the man, I took the clay pipe, pretended to smoke, and observed the sea of people streaming through the Brandenburger Tor. It would be the first time I saw my father cry, which left an infinitely stronger impression than the hundreds of bodies dancing on a ruin. Shortly after the wall fell, we left Berlin. When I told my teacher that I was moving to Frankfurt she asked, "which one, Main or Oder?" Since I wasn't sure, she assumed Oder, the "newly freed" city to the east. She was wrong. As most Berliners did at the time, we took pieces from the wall with us. I have lost my stones in the many moves that followed. Occasionally I have nightmares that my eulogy will simply be a hand-drawn map with random dots and lines, and atop my grave some jagged gray stones, remnants of *Mauer*. It is not entirely clear what these dreams say about my existence, but they are related, I am certain, to my love of archives, the ripe underworld.

After my linguistics seminar, I usually walk to the river that continues to separate the two towns. At this border, the archives bloom in cemeteries, abandoned control houses, the chips of paint from weathered bridges. After a few weeks crossing back and forth, I stumble upon the Archive of Human Destinies, with over one thousand life stories collected, shelved in stacks in the basement of the Collegium Polonicum, which faces the Polish embankment of the Oder. The archive is dedicated to the daily lives of people living on both sides of the river, oral histories that remember existence during the last one hundred years on this stretch of land. To imagine the land divided into countries, but also as part of the bodies who lived within smallest perimeters, inside surveilled identities, and upon the ruins of violent times.

I read for weeks in this subterranean sea of paper, photographs, and silence. The stories collected in binders, shift anonymous history to something akin to a star map, constellations made up of many singular lights that illumine the root tunnels upon which I sway. In this basement and behind each sentence "history" emerges in small incremental remains, a momentary gasp in the long exhale of time. Long after I ascend the stairs, coming up for air, the folders left behind on the table where I had sat hunched, I can still feel the hum below my feet.

WAR

Franz was a cow herder and all day long took cows to the river and back home to the farms. At one of the farms he met a young Polish boy around fifteen years old. He also met a Russian farmhand about sixteen years old and a Serbian officer about thirty-five years old. They all got along wonderfully. Franz and the Polish boy became friends. He was also a cow herder. Their main topic of conversation was the approach of the front and the hope that the Nazi regime would end. His Russian improved quickly. One evening, as he was returning home to the village with the animals, he passed a house and heard a voice call his name. The windows were latticed and had been remodeled into a prison. He turned around and saw through the window his Polish friend, who called out to him: "The Nazi pigs imprisoned me. Please, can you help me?" Franz said, "Yes, I will come back tonight and help you." He returned with tools, a hammer and tongs, which he handed to his friend through the window. When he passed with his cows the next morning, he saw a lot of police surrounding the village prison. They had dogs and kept calling: "The Pole is gone, the Pole is gone." His friend had urged him not to tell anybody, not even his mother. Franz was content about his friend's escape. When he had passed him the tools through the window he urged his friend to flee. To this day he does not know whether his friend survived his escape or the war. Franz was nine years and ten months old.

***

Walter's father was very intent on living discreetly in the city. He disagreed with Hitler. His parents, Walter's grandparents, had sent him away from Poland because he was born small and deformed. He found a job during the 1930s, yet it was all just temporary until the next unemployment period. When the war began, Polish forced laborers appeared in the city. Walter's father began visiting some of them. They lived in a concrete silo. Walter could not imagine what it was like to live like that. He did not suffer because he was half Polish. He loved his father, a very kind man. No one ever said anything negative about his Polish heritage. Never directly. What was much more difficult was his family's poverty, which made him an outsider. His father, for example, cut the children's hair with a razor. Everything came off at once. At school Walter's teachers were enthusiastic followers of Hitler. They would start to recount how many bombs had been dropped onto London before the class even started. The teachers also constantly beat him and his siblings. During breaks other students would bully them. His father was protective and also quite weighed down by all of this, especially when the Germans occupied Poznan, the city of his birth. Once he went to see his favorite sister in Stolice, close to Poznan. He never talked about that visit.

***

Achim was five years old when his family took a trip to the Polish border in the early 1930s. When they arrived, they saw on one side a German border official and on the other a Polish border official. They talked by the turnpike. His father addressed the German, and the Pole greeted them in Polish. Achim did not understand what he said but the Pole looked exactly like him. He was disappointed. He thought that Poles had a different skin color or some other feature that marked them as foreign. His mother started to pick flowers in no man's land and was politely told that she no longer stood on German ground. Years later, he sat in a tram wearing a Hitler youth uniform and saw an older man standing hunched over. As he had been taught, he got up to make space for the elderly man to sit. The man looked at him sadly, moved the briefcase that he had been holding in front of his chest to the side, and Achim saw the Star of David on his jacket. The classification of Jews was in that moment brought to his consciousness. A woman took the empty seat. Years later in Dachau, after the German capitulation, US soldiers explained to him, in a drastic manner, what had happened. He and his soldier comrades had to go into the shower rooms. The door was slammed shut with a loud bang. Steam started to rise from the showerheads. Until then they hadn't taken the film material seriously, but in the showers they panicked, convinced that they would be gassed. When they were finally let out, the US soldiers grinned at them.

***

Hermann's parents were close friends with many Polish families. Later, his mother was often accused of her former life in Poland. "Well, Käthe was particularly at ease in Poland." Table manners were more relaxed. People would hand over the butter with a knife stuck to it. Some smoked between dinner courses. His mother liked to smoke. She was a very attractive woman and often dazzled guests. In photographs you see a content and glowing face. She loved to celebrate and be festive. As a government official you were allowed to have visitors. When his grandparents, uncle, and aunt came from Berlin to visit Lodz, something happened that he still does not fully understand now. The whole family took a carriage wagon and drove through the ghetto. In a carriage wagon, with a Polish driver and all dressed up, they drove through the "attraction of Lodz." A few days later the glass plate on top of the living room table broke into many pieces. This was seen as a bad omen. If the glass plate breaks without reason something horrible is about to happen. Shortly after, the one hundred days of terror began. He remembers the date, January 20, 1945. His mother struggled with a handmade box, filling it with precious belongings. A Catholic nunnery took them in but the village was evacuated so they left on a classic trek by foot with a cart and a stroller. It was terribly cold. There was no longer a street and they had to take the frozen river Oder for their escape route. First they didn't even know where to go. They just followed the trek. The march along the Oder began past Breslau. They slept in the beds of strangers, in abandoned houses, and lit someone else's stove.

At dawn they began walking until it was dark again. Close to Schweidnitz they had first contact with the German armed forces that put them on open train wagons. The armed forces demanded that this baby, Hermann's brother, could not stay with them any longer. The soldiers said: "You can't be responsible for him anymore. We will take him to a hospital, when everything is over you get him back." His mother replied that this was out of the question and decided immediately to separate from the trek. They rode on a postal truck full of letters. The letters were not in bags but loose, like potatoes. They used them as blankets. At some point the train stopped, a voice yelled: "The Russians are here." His mother never spoke about the escape. It was the worst episode of her life. She experienced a social degradation, from a lively woman protected by her society to one in a thin coat with frozen feet, in daily struggle to survive. His father stayed behind in Lodz but had given his mother some poison. Perhaps he wanted to give her the option to die, to save his wife and family from the Russians. Did he give her a lower dose on purpose? Or maybe his mother asked him for the poison. It's hard to say. There's a blank space here, something he really doesn't know. He doesn't know if his mother had the poison or whether his father had given it to her during their first reunion, once they arrived in Berlin. He only remembers that she said: "Now we will sleep for a very long time." It's the last thing he can recall. The poison caused a prolonged loss of consciousness. He was the first to wake up. He saw his brother, mother, and grandmother lying on the floor. It was broad daylight. They weren't dead but in a kind of trance state. The adults swayed and staggered for a long time. His mother and grandmother could not control the movement of their eyes. The nerve influence was substantial. It is hard to say how long they were lying there. One day? Two? This topic was taboo in the family. Nobody would ever talk about it afterwards. To this day he cannot tolerate snow-covered landscapes. The image of his escape from Lodz to Berlin has impressed upon him a most existential sense of threat. When there is a winter without snow he is glad. He gets very depressed when he sees snow. Snow, to him, signals catastrophe.

***

Erwald was born on October 25, 1932, in Langenbielau, Slesia (today Bielawa). His family was removed in May of 1947. There were no SS units stationed in the city, but he can remember the night from the 8th to the 9th of May 1945; they had to constantly change flags. When the SS marched past, they had to hang out their swastika flags. When the Russians came, they let the white flag fly. The lilac was in full bloom. Langenbielau was known for the weavers' protest in 1848, a communist act. The Russians felt connected to this place and Germans remained relatively unscathed. As long as the Russians protected them they were well off, but when the Poles took over the administration they lost their rights. As Germans they had to carry white armbands and give up their house. They packed their most important belongings and left. It must have been around *Johannisnacht*, during solstice, and they celebrated by making little wooden ships with flower wreaths and candles, setting them to sail on the river. These wreaths served as guides through their fate. A lot of their goods were stolen during the long march, and when he arrived in Frankfurt Oder he was only carrying a small backpack. At the border crossing, by the river, everyone took off their armbands and threw them into the current.

**

RIVER

Summer cradles the street. When we cross the river between the twin cities, the linguistics professor assures me: "You will find something here. For women the spaces begin to open. Look, over there, can you see the beavers?" We pass the dead river arm. I feel that she is only able to say these words outside of rooms and in passing. The street signs are now in Polish. We walk towards the dormitories. Sometimes people drowned in the river in an attempt to cross. The chart that I keep for the bridge crossing in the coming months highlights the weather (usually raining), traffic, and emotions. That night, sleeping in Poland, I dream of a type of crying.

Odra in Polish means "river." *Oder* in German means "or." The current not just as water but also as history of the human spirit. For some the river is famous, marking a world that began at Yalta. Behind its name one can also trace the collapse of East Germany. After 1989 the word "Oder" became synonymous with smuggling, trafficking, nightclubs, twilight business. Today one can observe at its banks badgers and herons. During prehistoric glacial melting periods it began its course along the sediments of moraines.

GDR

Susanne

I grew up on Bergstrasse, where a lot of fugitives first landed, mostly from regions east of the Oder. Many former Frankfurters, who fled in 1945, never came back. We belonged to the ones that did. There were people from the East who talked about the old homeland, a constant topic of conversation on staircases and among families. And yet, to this whole area the eastern region remained a fairyland. People mentioned the German city names, but we, as school children, only ever learned the Polish names and never quite put these realities together. For example, we once drove with our teacher to Sagan and Sorau. He mentioned Polish and German city names. I remembered a stanza from a poem that I had learned. "Tell me child, so rough the wind, how many cities this must have been"—or along those lines. The towns belonged to a dream world. Only after the border opened again, one could see that they truly existed. . . . We lived with my grandparents here in Frankfurt. My grandfather was a social democrat and had an enormous influence on me. He came from a simple family. He was a mason and had been part of important building initiatives in the 1920s. He exposed me from a young age to books. Shakespeare and Goethe. He belonged to the kind of person who taught himself. At the dinner table he would read *Faust* to us or *Hermann and Dorothea*, *Julius Caesar*. We liked to listen to him. When we read *Macbeth* in school I was disappointed. I later realized that it was a great piece, but our teacher did not have my grandfather's ability to speak language directly from the heart. . . . Ideological ideas only started to come back into focus around 1950. That's when we began to learn more about the "socialist character." I remember in 1953 when Stalin died and we all had to stand together in silence to remember him. Many teachers actually cried, but several of the older students could not hide their laughter. They were kicked out of school. At home we always talked a lot about the past, and as children we were very interested in these stories. During the 1920s some of my relatives had gone to Berlin. The young girls went as housemaids. My grandfather's sisters and his brother went too, and our family entertained many stories about their time in the city. Berlin had been such a prosperous place that even though my relatives were poor, they were able to regularly go on trips and frequent the theater. Many of these stories were not GDR "conforming" but they lived on anyway. . . . I experienced the event of the border closure as terrible. The view to the outside world was now completely obstructed. I wanted to travel. On the other hand there were a lot of people, to whom I also belonged, that said now we have to do something productive. It was always my longing that something valuable would come out of this country. . . . I can't really say that we had any worries in the '60s and '70s. Our life was simple and took place on a low material level. Nobody could purchase a big car. Everyone knew you had to order your Trabi eight years in advance, but compared to what my grandparents told me about the war period and what we experienced during the postwar period, where you could freeze to death in your own home, we lived well. We were privileged and had a wonderful apartment. That was one of the most valuable goods in the GDR. For the first time in my life I had a bathtub with some heating. It was a modest two-bedroom place with a small kitchen. I must say we never really worried, regardless of how much or how little money was there at the end of the month. . . .

It was around 1985. I remember this very clearly. I was forty-five years old and worked on a house opposite the University Viadrina. I sat with some of my colleagues in one of the house's most beautiful rooms. It was a fairly big office. I looked at this stunning building that was also home to the district council. There were flowers; the sunlight flooded through the windows. It was a great working space. Suddenly, I caught myself thinking, here you will sit until you are retired and only then will you be able to go visit the West. As a GDR citizen you could officially go west at the age of sixty. I thought about my aunt who would be long dead by then. My longing was there despite all the beauty I had.

Gerda

When I was in eleventh grade the school director said to me, "Fräulein you will not study. The school does not recommend you for higher learning. You are a precarious candidate. The state puts so much money into universities and you will be one of the first who will take off for West Berlin." This was a problem back then. Every year people left in droves to go to West Berlin. The director suspected that I would leave too. As you can see he was wrong. . . . There was the so-called "Human Resources Office" in East Berlin. You went there to find work. I didn't quite know what I wanted to do. I was sixteen. I had a boyfriend. He lived in Babelsberg and studied at the film school. He advised me to try and find work in television, which was just starting in the East. So when I went to the office I said: "I would like a job in television." I imagined becoming a production assistant or floor manager, but I was told everything was already taken. I have thrown a temper tantrum three times in my life. This was the first time. I left the office and after an hour went back to stand in line again. "I told you that there is nothing available," the woman said to me. I replied: "I thought that something would have freed up by now." "No," she said, "there is no work for you in television." I went back outside and stood in line for a third time. When the secretary saw me again, she laughed and gave me application materials. The job title was "studio assistant." I was thrilled. During my interview I was asked about my interests, but then cut short and told that I would be working in the technical department. That was really the worst. I had no interest in technical matters. I wanted to make art. I did learn to enjoy the work. There wasn't much being broadcast, for lunch a test film and some news item in the evening. That was usually it. This meant very irregular working hours for which I was thankful.... On August 12, 1961, I returned home from my night shift. On my way home, I saw a well-known journalist who was drunk and slurred: "Tonight.... tonight the border will be closed." I did not take him seriously. I thought he may want to rhyme a song, it sounded so pleasant. I went home but I could not fall asleep. The possibility of a closure did not leave me. I asked a friend of mine, who often took his dog for a walk at night, to pass by Nordbahnhof, another crossing, and see if the there was any activity. He assured me that the area was completely deserted; everything was calm. There was no one. I went to sleep. During the night the TV station called me. There was a special broadcast on the closing of the border from the GDR to West Berlin.... The second time in my life that I lost my temper was at the housing office. My apartment with two bedrooms had become too small, and in exchange for my place I was offered another apartment that belonged to an old woman who lived in the Scharnhorststrasse. The housing office, however, refused to permit the exchange because I was not married. H was, at this point, in Poland. I called him and yelled down the line if he wanted to get married or not. He immediately returned to Berlin and we got married in

January of '66. The best part of living on Scharnhorststrasse was walking along the borderline. No one can imagine how close we lived to that line. . . . The drama surrounding the Wolf Biermann affair happened in 1976. During a concert tour to West Germany the GDR retracted his citizenship and he was not allowed to come back. My husband signed, alongside other authors, a protest petition. Two days later my supervisor called me into his office and demanded that I distance myself in a written statement from my husband's position. The following day I returned to the office and told my supervisor that I was not going to distance myself from anything. He threatened to suspend me. I went home and suffered a nervous breakdown. . . . Solidarność and Kuroń were very important to us. We admired the Poles because they continued to go on strike whenever food prices increased, for example, before Christmas. We kept wondering what was wrong with the Germans. Why did they just accept these conditions? Neighbors disappeared overnight and we often contemplated whether we should apply for a travel visa. There used to be this saying "DDR: Der dumme Rest" (The dumb remain*).* We all knew the GDR was finished. Pensioners were, of course, allowed to go west and they often turned that into a second professional career. They departed with long shopping lists and for some extra money returned with goods. My mother would hide items in her underwear, always terrified that she would get pulled out when crossing the bunker of tears. When she died, H, my daughter, and I were allowed to go to West Berlin for the first time together. There was a small inheritance. My daughter went to Norway and H and I went to England. This had been my dream.

I really wanted to stay there. I spent my remaining money on a fur coat that was three sizes too big for me. I thought when I am sixty-five, in about fifteen years, I will be much fatter and an old person gets cold quickly. So I got this coat, which was actually quite cheap. Then I bought a sewing machine, a few small items, and gifts for my friends. When we returned, I crossed at Sandkrugbrücke. I cannot tell you how difficult the one hundred meter-long way back home to the Scharnhorststrasse was. I just sobbed. I thought this is it. In the next ten years I will not be able to go west again. Every step felt unbearable. I pulled my luggage behind me. I must have looked so pitiful, even the customs officer was alarmed. I could not talk or be talked to for three days. . . . When the wall came down we took a train west. We did the usual; H gave the conductor some money and we were given a sleeper. At the border, friendly patrol guards greeted us. The same patrol guards who had called us cannibals in the past were now unrecognizable. One of them smiled at me. This sudden change was the worst possible thing I could imagine. I am sure he was a good man, but to me this smile indicated absolute horror.

Gerta

Even as a child I loved order. There was a rhododendron bush, which my mother tended carefully, awaiting its blooming each year. One morning, she noticed that I had plucked the blossoms and planted them in a perfect circle around the bush. Another time, after a bomb attack in front of the cellar's window, I found decapitated chicken heads and proceeded to arrange them into a straight line. When we were asked to collect old clothes for school, I was ashamed of carrying such a bundle. My mother had to do that for me.

My father was a generous but a very impractical man. Not even my mother, who was extremely practical, could change that. He went everywhere by foot to hold services. He wanted to help with the potato harvest after the war but his hand became infected. I loved my father very much; however, he did not believe in resisting authorities. This was also true for the Nazi ideology. He did not understand the danger that was approaching. My mother was more critical. She despised people who explained Jewish removal by claiming they had died from pneumonia. In our house Russians slept not in beds or on the floor but on the stove. As a child I found that very funny. I remember one of the children sitting on the lap of a Russian who was playing with a broken telephone. The

Russian kept saying: "Hello, hello, Hitler here. . . ." During my university studies in math I was one of a handful of women in the entire department. The men lived in the city. I lived somewhere entirely different. Once during winter we even had snow on our beds. I had to get coal from the train station and often experienced homesickness, crying on the bridge where you could see the train tracks that lead out of Greifswald. As a child I was often called "tear jar," because whenever my mother would read us a story I became sad even before the story indicated any kind of tragedy. I would take my little sitting bench, placed it in front my mother's legs, and then lay my head in her lap so that no one would see my tears. . . . A roommate of mine didn't like to go to classes and instead would read these amazing tomes, *Gone with the Wind* and so on. She would slip underneath her beige blanket with rose motifs and excuse herself claiming she had kidney pain. I was known for my careful note taking and she simply read through those notes and passed the test. The other girls and I, in exchange, read her books at night. It was this roommate who also kept saying to me: "In two years we will study medicine, you and I . . . ." I worked briefly as a laboratory intern at a Christian hospital. My father had arranged that for me, and unfortunately also agreed that I wouldn't get paid for the position. We worked even Saturdays, cleaning slides with toothbrushes. I worked in the pediatrics ward, which was very difficult. The children were afraid of glowworms that kept flying against the window and it was hard to calm them down. I worked week after week as the night nurse. After one of my shifts, I cycled to Brandenburg, in secret, to take the entrance exam to become a medical assistant and was accepted. . . . My biggest passion during those years was going to the *Komische Oper*. My classmates made fun of me for my hobby but that did not bother me. When I received a good grade, I rewarded myself with an opera ticket. When I received a bad grade, I comforted myself with an opera ticket. I did my practical training at the Lutherstift in Frankfurt Oder and chose gynecology. Not my dream field. I began to work with Frau Doktor S. and we were responsible for eighty beds. We worked around the clock and often performed our first surgeries at dawn. Frau Doktor had worked at the Charité hospital in Berlin during the war and operated amidst bomb attacks and air raids. She was known to never take her boots off. In fact, she never went home at all. I lived in this little house that was centrally located on the hospital grounds. It allowed me to get to the surgery and delivery room quickly. I no longer went to the *Komische Oper*. During my first year at the Lutherstift I became very sick. I had terrible stomach cramps and some of my colleagues thought I wanted to avoid my final exams. Frau Doktor examined me and sent me immediately to the operating room. It turned out that I had two tumors on my ovaries that kept turning, causing the pain. To prove it, Frau Doktor came to me the next morning, after the operation, with my uterus and ovaries in a bowl. She wanted to assure me that it was not cancer. I was only thirty-one years old. I was glad the pain receded. It would have been impossible to work at the hospital if I had a husband or a child. I was always on call. No one really had a private life. On several occasions I was called in the middle of the night and arrived in my nightgown. . . . A terrible incident occurred during Palm

Sunday in 1974. I suddenly noticed, while asleep, that someone was holding on to my lower arm. The way my mother would sometimes wake us. Yet, this wasn't a dream. Someone had broken into the house and now sat on my bed. When I tried to get up a man hit me and tried to suffocate me. Until then, I believed I was stronger than any man, but I could not free myself of him. When he tried to rape me, I suddenly remembered my mother's advice to say that I was sick, if anyone ever assaulted me. I told him I had a sexually transmittable disease, and he immediately got up and disappeared. Later, I noticed that he had taken my money and purse. I have a strong voice but no one would have heard me. I called the pastor. I couldn't remember the emergency number. It took a long time before the police arrived. I could not describe the intruder. I had only seen his silhouette. I laughed when I saw the dog that was supposed to find him. He was not the brightest. The police sent me to the hospital to document the throat marks. The first thing they asked me was whether I had my SV card on me, which of course I didn't. Frau Doktor only heard of the events the next morning. The investigation fizzled out. They found nothing. Eventually, I moved to the same hospital floor as Frau Doktor. During my time at the hospital Frau Doktor and I, nurse E., and her son always ate together. When we were asked to move, Frau Doktor suggested we all live together. We found a large apartment. Sundays we sat in the large live-in kitchen drinking coffee all afternoon. After 1988 I lived alone with Frau Doktor in the apartment. When I came home I could always sit down to a warm meal. We lived very healthily but against my will. No butter, no rolls, only ham and sour milk that she made herself. Occasionally some fruit; never anything sugary. I was once asked by a colleague, after congratulating Frau Doktor to her birthday, why I still called her "Frau Doktor" after all these years. When I told Frau Doktor this anecdote, she just said: "Who cares" . . . . My mother died very consciously. She planned everything with precision. Each female grandchild received a necklace. I sat the entire night at her bedside. She died in the early morning, around the break of dawn, but at six my shift started and I left. I was needed for a surgery. When I returned she lay dead in my room. . . . In 1997 I became very ill and had to undergo chemotherapy. Frau Doktor was also increasingly immobilized. I lost my hair and stopped working. She refused to go to the hospital to the very end and only spent her last three days there. She died on January 27, 1998. After my long illness my love for the opera was rekindled. One of the singers from the '50s still occasionally performed. I often brought him flowers, and I could finally redeem what I had missed with my mother and Frau Doktor. In 2005, I drove every day to Berlin and visited the dying singer. His last twelve days I was able to take care of him around the clock. He wanted to build a monument in my honor and out of gratitude. When I asked him whether he would build it with stone or wood, he replied, "nothing but gold."

NOTEBOOK

In the basement of the apartment where I am staying two boxes remain. They are filled with photographs, notebooks, some clothes. Things I did not take with me when I left Germany and that, in some measure, are supposed to signal an anchor here, a remaining presence. Two boxes I will not give up.

I practiced a return some years ago when I decided to go on a long walk across the European continent. I wanted to feel its landscape again. Feel its language rhythms coo me to sleep.

A few months before I went on the long walk, I woke one night from a dream, or maybe it was just a noise. As soon as I woke, I lost my sense of gravity, shot up to the ceiling and could not get back into the distant body below. As "I" was caught below the stucco, I realized this experience was an aspect of dying. That dying was awful and disorienting. No containment, specter, or periphery. A placeless drift.

The walk started at Land's End in Galicia, once the furthest borders of known world, snaked along the Pyrenees and ended in Berlin, where I met with one of my oldest friends, Nina, who had grown up on the other side of the wall from me.

We walked the former East-West division, along ruins, placards, and portraits of the deceased. The actual notebook I had with me at the time is now almost illegible and, quite frankly, incomprehensible. I wrote down street names, places where the wall once stood, the names of the dead who failed to cross, and sketched swans under bridges. Sometimes remains of the wall lurked in the landscape; sometimes we had to imagine it with the help of various maps. In the end most vivid were the fragments of conversation that ebbed and flowed. Fragments, which I jotted down hurriedly, that blended with the sounds of our feet touching surfaces.

Wannnsee, Berlin

I tell you about my dream. My first memory light. How I followed it. How it followed itself. Prompting. We pass Peacock Island where the King of Prussia sent his alchemist and other exotic animals. On the shore an old man behind a gate screams in bird voices. Later the zoos brought their animals here too. With weeping willows. He shakes the gate. A dragonfly rests on spikes. You tell me about your dream. You are in a prison with him, with only one key to this prison. We eat Soljanka. You are endlessly wired. Cigarettes and long legs carry you straight to the lake where you strip and scare lame ducks with your splash. I sit tired by the reeds. The nothing that saves itself.

Bornholmer Strasse, Berlin

Do you have an answer to all that you choose? The city, its predilection: soft margarine and see-through milk but not during Tschernobyl. Long naps. My island life. I wished you here. A sister. Never had moss but covered surfaces and sweet snakes from the store.

In school you read Aitmatov's Dschamilla. *I, Goethe's* Faust. *When we both left the walled cities for a more provincial childhood, a friendly neighbor offered you a box filled with old amputated Barbie dolls. She said you could take one or two home. You threw them to the dogs. You chewed them up with the dogs.*

Teltow Canal, Berlin

The spontaneous decision to cross the frozen Teltow Canal. The area was brightly lit. Slid under and then crawled toward. Twenty-five meters before West Berlin. I can be peaceful, nobody can hurt me. I can be grateful, nobody can force me.

Sacrow, Berlin

We walk to Schloss Sacrow. The border ran across the church's precinct. The first time we met, we went swimming. Our faces shrank. Now we sit. Grass growing over the city. Our paws bleeding. The Prussian castle looks like a large house. Your eyes very tired almost fall asleep. If they had shot more precisely. You say. The ravens sit with the ducks. Even the Havel was split. Every separation is a link. We reach the end of its telling. In the small town where we would grow up together, further west, further south, a teacher once said "Berliner Göre." I had a narrow face and snot on both shirt arms. A sea of barley and large trees.

Nina, my friend, who grew upon the other side of the wall from me, returned permanently to our broken city, planted herself there, while I left for the mountains, for the sea, for the desert for the forest for the places I never dreamed to be. Carrying the weight across many lines, losing some, picking it back up again. Clouds racing over wheat stocks, casting brief shadows. I wrote and destroyed the writing, leveled the words into another tongue and became sleepless.

LANDFLUCHT

It is hot. The city has become an asphalt lake, a heat wave. Nina has been leasing a piece of land east of Berlin and we escape for the weekend. There is a dacha, rows of vegetables, plum trees. We build a fire, walk through the forest barefoot, and drink cheap wine. I get lost for a few moments in a field of sunflowers and lay myself on the ground. The smell of fall is encroaching, a moist darkness is already moving up from below, mixed with the smoke of our logs. Something angles towards the thicket, worms bulge from the soil. Wakeful sleepiness hangs over roofs. An abandonment, too. These towns in the east barely audible.

Later that evening we walk to the village to watch a special screening of a documentary about the East German writer Thomas Brasch. The screening is held in the local gym, complimentary hors d'oeuvres plates, crackers with cheese, are offered. The film threads along a live reading of Brasch's sister's intimate dialogue with her now dead brother. Am I imaging this or are people actually smoking inside the gym? We drink more wine. *Bleiben will ich, wo ich nie gewesen bin.* To stay where I have never been. A line from one of Brasch's poems, the title of the film, the evening, his life.

During a cold December in 1976, Brasch fled East Berlin, fled from Germany to Germany. After Brasch distributed flyers that critiqued the GDR regime, his father, a high-ranking functionary in the Sozialistischen Einheitspartei Deutschland (SED), denounced him to the Stasi and he was arrested. He spent some time in prison then worked as a cutter in a mill. In his diary he wrote, "We don't do anything else but work, eat, and sleep." His ambivalent relationship to the state blistered even further after the "Biermann affair," in which several GDR artists, including Christa Wolf and Nina Hagen, cosigned a letter in support of the singer. He left East Berlin shortly after, but not without trying to publish his first book there. It was rejected with the suggestion that he should leave the GDR altogether. In the West, Brasch quickly gained recognition and won prizes and money, but he remained *der Dichter vom Osten.* The media often taunted him to renounce his socialist upbringing and embrace the free market carousel to which he replied: "A writer's theme is not the land in which he lives but the problem that he has." He remained a stranger, longing for the country on the other side of the wall, his siblings, a return. Writing inside of this longing. Writing against both countries, the state. Writing plays, poems, films. When he received the Bavarian film prize for his film *Engel aus Eisen,* he stoically thanked the film school of the GDR. The Bavarians booed him. In his acceptance speech, he also declared his commitment to the contradictions of his times that he as an artist continues to lay bare and work within. Government officials who had praised his work a few minutes earlier awkwardly turned on the soles of their feet and listened with heads hanging low.

Red faced and sweaty. After the ceremony, the Bavarian state government wrote a letter. They no longer considered him a guest. He should pay for his own hotel bill, they demanded. The state sulked and Brasch's father, who had not talked to him for years, called him. The anarchic desire to tell one's own story on one's own terms. The underworld is perfect. *Wir sind ratlos mitternachts.* The relationship between father and son remained tense, filled with question marks. He returned only once for his fathers state funeral, marching band and politicians, the army guard saluting the mourning dissident. After the wall fell, Brasch began to write a novel. Thousands of pages that swelled on his desk for years. He kept throwing them out, rewriting, inserting himself only to release the "I," shortly after, from the plot again. He wrote, and drank, and his heart began to fail. Always bending towards a fog, peerless. The epic novel was finally released, a thin sunken book. . . .

Warum sind Sie Schriftsteller geworden?
Why did you become a writer?

Ich hatte die bestimmte Absicht?
I had a particular intention.

Welche Absicht denn?
What kind of intention?

Darueber spricht man nicht.
Of that one must not speak.

Nina states that she will never be able to return, even though we are sitting, right now, in the former East still East. Her country does not exist anymore, she says. Why is this important, doesn't the ground itself allow for some belonging, regardless of lines and names? Or does the return, its impossibility, signal nostalgia, longing for a different time, rather than a different place? We walk home with the smoky silence of the gym in our throats. Brasch's voice echoing along the empty streets and boarded up stores.

Wo ich bin will ich nicht bleiben aber
Where I am I don't want to stay but
Die ich liebe will ich nicht verlassen aber
The ones I love I don't want to leave but
Die ich kenne will ich nicht mehr sehen aber
The ones I know I don't want to see but
Wo ich lebe da will ich nicht sterben aber
Where I live I don't want to die but
Wo ich sterbe da will ich nicht hin in aber
Where I die I don't want to go but
Bleiben will ich wo ich nie gewesen bin
I want to stay where I have never been

POST-TRANSGRESSION SYNDROME

In the darkness of the room breathing. Mine. An old mouth sails through the air telling me a story so irrefutable it remains inconclusive. I am the inheritor of a story, the mouth grandiosely proclaims. A curse! Though it could also be considered a gift, depending on the perspective. The mouth does not dwell on this angle. Your ancestors were of the moving kind. Never voluntarily, of course. The mouth rubs its gums. They are inflamed. Your mother desired some of that lost ground. She married your father, who opened the gates to an old familiar land. Did it matter that it was Germany? The mouth seems unsure about the answer. Clears its throat. Your mother's father would never visit her there. It was the expelled place, the vacant shape. On this ground she would plant herself and her descendants firmly, swearing to never move again. Some twenty years later, you, her daughter, couldn't wait to leave, couldn't wait to expel yourself from a pain in your throat. Voluntarily, so it seemed. What began as innocuous pilgrimages to this and that place, was, in fact, already an enactment of the curse, of distance, inexplicable restlessness. Years came and went, and the map grew wider. It became more and more impossible to return to the ground. The mouth gasps, has a moment of clarity; it is a rehearsed moment. I know the script but listen intently. Now you wonder about this ground all the time, the mouth whispers. This land, where trains depart by the hour and the forest is muddy history, a rotten bagpipe. Everything is fear, and, here, rightness. You listen to snores, the little stone dwellings in the water, where Rhine Maidens and wild grasses hair-over hills. The mouth pauses, sighs. Is a little taken by its own lyric tendencies. This last part is always hard for the mouth. In the dark room gums bloom into red tulips. Avatars. Urge the mouth to continue. You would have been nobody here, the mouth eventually stutters. We both fall silent and I swallow the bitter sentence, as if the most natural remedy. Yes, the mouth is right. What we love we must be very far away from; loss is what must be enacted. Severance is the great locutor.

PILGRIMAGE

In the last pages of the notebook I had carried across Europe, I find a quote from Diogenes—*Solvitur ambulando* (It is resolved by walking)—crossed out. Followed by questions. *Why walk, why make the journey? The desire for a threshold, a movement away from myself, or to remember: we the crow, we the dirt? Scared or strong? Why is telling a story considered an act of love?*

When I crossed the Pyrenees by foot to Marseille, I did not visit Walter Benjamin's grave in Portbou because I did not know then that he was buried there. It is only several years later that I learn of Benjamin's route: Paris, Marseille, Lourdes, Banyuls-sur-Mer, Portbou, and realize it echoed my own in reverse. At the very end of this road, crossing the Pyrenees, walking from west to east, I decided to go north up the coast, and therefore not to the little sea town where Benjamin is buried in a Catholic cemetery under the name Benjamin Walter.

While in Marseille, Benjamin met Hannah Arendt and obtained a visa from the US consulate. After taking the train to Port-Vendres, he and several others decided on a small path across the mountains that eventually wound down into the small town of Portbou. A steep and difficult route. The only way to enter Spain clandestinely.

On the afternoon of September 24, Lisa Fittko, Walter Benjamin, Henny Gurland and her son Joseph made a discreet survey of the track. Benjamin, too tired to go back to Banyuls, decided to stay all night on the mountainside and start the climb again from there in the morning. He spent the night alone in a little stand of pine trees. At dawn on the morning of September 25, Lisa, Henny, and Joseph set out on the path to meet up again with Benjamin. "Azéma had impressed upon us: Leave before sunrise, mingle with the vineyard workers, take nothing with you . . . and don't speak! The term 'path' gradually proved to be an exaggeration. Now and then there was a path to be seen, but increasingly it was just a barely recognizable gravelly track between boulders. Until we came to the steep vineyard, which I can never forget." From there, the road became a clamber over rocks up the shady side of the mountain. Benjamin had calculated that, given his state of health, he would have to stop every ten minutes and rest for one, a resolution he strictly adhered to, concentrating on his watch and his rests. On the last stretch his companions had to help him. After several hours, they got to the top of the ridge. "Finally we reached the summit. I had gone on ahead and I stopped to look around. The spectacular scene appeared so unexpectedly that for a moment I thought I was seeing a mirage . . . the deep-blue Mediterranean. . . ." At this point Lisa Fittko said goodbye. This, her first crossing of the route on which she was to accompany so many other refugees. The rest of the party followed the path down into Portbou.

Hannah Arendt noted Benjamin's unfortunate timing: "One day earlier Benjamin would have got through without any trouble; one day later the people in Marseilles would have known that for the time being it was impossible to pass through Spain. Only on that particular day was the catastrophe possible." He was either slightly too late or too early. Once he arrived in Portbou he stayed at the Hotel de Francia, where he died on September 27, 1940, age forty-eight, from a morphine overdose after being refused entry into Spain and passage out of Europe.

In *Walter Benjamin's Grave*, Michael Taussig traces the receipt issued to the deceased man after he had turned himself over to the Spanish police, who had, only a day prior, received orders to send all refugees back to occupied France. The receipt lists "five lemon sodas, four telephone calls, dressing of the corpse plus disinfection of his room, the washing and whitening of the mattress." Another receipt is made out to a carpenter in Portbou who built the cloth-lined coffin.

Arendt would later visit the small cemetery and claim that she found nothing. Gershom Scholem would call the gravesite "fake." Taussig, in his own version of Benjamin's last days, decries the cult of the dead, its tragedy overshadowing the writer's work before detailing his own pilgrimage to Portbou, to Benjamin's grave, and his desire to absorb something of the "dead man, the holy man."

I did not visit Benjamin's grave, nor did I think of him while walking through the border towns of the Pyrenees. Instead, a constant feeling of pain subsumed me, both physical (knees, breathless, almost vertical mountain routes) as well as spiritual; death in summer is everywhere squinting awkwardly, a white vacant glare. The heat was oppressive and all that mattered was water, eventually. It is true that after days of walking in such thick layers of air one wonders about the dead below one's feet, whole cultures swallowed into the mountainside, little forlorn crosses barely withstanding the wind. The road appeared as vocation, as first memory. I could not find a line, a border. It was all crags, all swarm, all knees burning. I never knew exactly whether I was in Spain or France or somewhere altogether different. It is only now, thousands of miles away and in dark winter temperatures, that I can write these words and insert Benjamin's gravestone epigraph as a final breath to the walk. At the cemetery, the glass memorial, atop steps that lead away from the land and down to the sea, his words fracture in the light:

It is more arduous to honor the memory of the nameless than that of the renowned. Historical construction is dedicated to the memory of the nameless.

OYNEG SHABBES

On November 9, 2016, a few months after visiting the basements, the river that is a border and freshly returned to the desert, I will listen to Jewish survivors in reflection of Kristallnacht's seventy-eight anniversary, a hot morning in southern Arizona. A woman next to me will weep. *We made it to the Belarusian border. My mother's breast milk had dried up.*

On the eve of the election, the Kristallnacht anniversary, and also the date that the wall opened twenty-seven years ago, I will drive in my car along the outskirts of Tucson and listen to the radio. The highway empty. None of my students would show up. *We made it to the Volga River. The Germans bombed the train and except for one car, we traveled on.* I will not go to the poet's lecture two days later. The air suddenly turning. Wind will lambast the garden. *And when I was sick and helpless, I prayed to my God.*

My middle school students, the next day, some of whom just arrived in this country, will tell me about their dreams. They will hold onto their brightly colored, placid folders and sit at little round tables. Tables at which my students live, think, and are afraid. My Congolese student will recount his nightmare. He is in a vast jungle. A young black girl appears.

She calls his name several times. He wakes up, drinks some water. When he goes back to sleep, the girl is there again, in the jungle, except now she is dead.

Others will speak of nuns holding knives, of great grandparents, black snakes, soldiers holding them down while they cry: "I am dying, I am dying." Some will dream of angels. Some of a sea made of chocolate where the chocolate chips are rocks. The student that got hit by a car, with a slow healing scar on his forehead, does not want to write about dreams, doesn't even look at me.

When ground swells all eyes go under.

The historical destination of humans is unclear to themselves, Alain Badiou will say on November 9, 2016. His advice: "Go beyond the world as it is."

In the heat of this November, the desert will sound on. People who live here will begin to look like ancient desert roses. Their skin taut and eyes clear, crystalline, embedded in deep-lying holes. The human skin peeled toward an ancient seabed. The narrative always one of endurance, of making do, of staying close to the ground. Clocks will melt; their hands and numbers vanish. White cramped shells will whirl about the night.

In my dreams: fractures of other places, shabby apartment viewings in Berlin. In my blood: the memory of the worst possible outcome. In my skin: the tender coil of human will gone violent. The curve of my spine indicates the many hundreds of years listening up late at night for the mortal threat.

The night before Thanksgiving, a Wednesday, Robert will perform *INTERNAL*. An adaption of Leyb Goldin's "Chronicle of a Single Day" composed, buried, and exhumed in the Warsaw Ghetto. . . .

The opposite table is already in a state of grace. Peaceful quietness, they are already eating. And it somehow seems to you that the people at that table feel superior to you, worthier. And it hasn't reached your table yet. And you are only imagining it: somehow the people sitting here have such long faces, not-having-eaten faces, with swollen ghetto spots under their eyes, which give the face a look.

"Chronicle of a Single Day" is a text that was buried as part of the Oyneg Shabbes archive, which sought to document the experiences of the Jewish ghetto in Poland. Deep into the ground of the ghetto, notes, plays, sketches in tins and jars, were lowered into unmarked earth for some afterlife. Despite the knowledge of the Shoah's radical erasure that would soon meet them, these writers and archivists, in an underground collective sense, held the innate belief that "nothing was unimportant."

Here there is no sunrise. The day comes to the door like a beggar. The days are already shorter. But I . . . I like the autumnal foggy dawns. Everything becomes so dreamy, lost in thought, longing, concentrated in itself. Everything draws away . . . people, world, cloud prepares for something that connects . . . The grey patch standing in the corner of the room with open arms, that's the new day.

CEMETERY

A few blocks from the basement of the Collegium Polonicum and its archive where I read every day instead of preparing for my linguistics seminar, the Jewish cemetery lies overgrown. It is now a forested area. No indication of a cemetery anywhere. Some tarps flutter in the wind. A local historian fills in the silence and tells me about the vanished graveyard, shows me some surviving documents. Burials were recorded as early as 1399. The first non-Jewish cemetery caretaker took over its maintenance duties in 1870. His grandson, who continued the family tradition and even lived on the grounds, was, in 1941, under pressure from the German government forced to take a leave of absence. He spent a short time in a labor camp but was quickly released due to illness. Despite prohibitions issued by the Gestapo, he continued to look after the cemetery. Later he wrote: "In 1941, 110 young people were buried. The corpses all came from a labor camp in Finkenheerd, close to Frankfurt Oder. The dead almost all came from Lodz. Horrible how these corpses looked, starved and broken apart. . . . I once asked a young Jewish man 'How is it that so many children are dying?' And he responded: 'If they want that someone dies, then they die.'"

After a bombing of Frankfurt Oder in February of 1944 he noted: "Roof off, several windows and doors gone. But I was able to rearrange the morgue fairly well again." He documented the last official burial on December 11, 1944. The prominent doctor was one of the few Jews at the time that received a gravestone. "Officially I was not allowed to be there. Some people from the city had orders to bury him somewhere close to a path, but I was able to circumvent that." The caretaker also recited Kaddish for women who passed away during a time when there was no one in Frankfurt Oder who could have undertaken proper Jewish burial rites.

In the 1960s, while the border briefly opened, some high-ranking SED party members decided the city needed more beds. A hotel with a parking lot was built on the former cemetery grounds. Locals took the burial stones and used them for their own needs. Some were later found in Catholic churches and by the river embankment.

The remaining slabs, I am told, are the traces of a former funhouse called Eden, which had views to the water.

Further up, patches of nettles where once the mourning hall stood.

***

Upon my return to the desert we will drive, a group of six in a minivan, to a small abandoned cemetery in Douglas, Cochise County. The cemetery was gifted to the Jewish History Museum and we are to investigate what this gift might mean. The cemetery lies a few yards away from the border wall, off of a dirt road, counting around twelve graves. The graves are slabs of cement, some with headstones, others without. A decaying fence marks the circumference, the edges of the burial site. Several of the slabs were moved from their original setting, which will cause me to wonder where the dead actually are. Do they care about our discussions, ideas to install a newly welded iron gate, a plaque that would describe Jewish burial rites, or the formation of local partnerships for quarterly visits of the grounds? And yet, I will also remember that taking care of the dead in these ways, though it may actually express a caretaking of a relationship that exists outside of the cemetery, is important. We subsist as leaflets, as plums dropped to the ground. The statues in the distance might be called liberty, memorial, or Mexico. In the past, kids have come to the cemetery to light bonfires, graffiti the slabs, and to cool off at night.

Anastasia will meet us at the entrance of the cemetery. She lives close by, on a homestead, skirting the small farming community of Elfrida. During our first visit to her homestead several years ago, the goats exited through the front door. Turkeys greeted us at the gate. Over by the fence a pile of bones, some nests in the tree. We heard the cranes fly in from the west. The house inside had barely any furniture, reminded me of a cottage in the French countryside, eternally cold walls and exceptional cheeses waiting.

Across from the main house lay the remains of a private museum once a caretaking facility for the dying. The spiny beds now covered with large pumpkin heads. We passed below some pig hind. The animals followed, sometimes on top of everything. Open fields all around. In the summer they become havens to some of the most poisonous snakes in the country. It is a winded and dusty land with failing wells. We drove through the Dragoon Mountains. The road forked next to a large grain tower, next to a border patrol checkpoint. Silence here, I have noticed, indicates a thicket, a paragon. The dead goat still rotting through layers of soil. Deer carcasses appearing in a merry entanglement. When we sat down to cheese and bread I wondered how I would cope if I lived here. Anastasia's days seemed to move along unpredictable rhythms, anchored by specific rituals and chores. Each day its own palette. No exchanges except with herself and the animals, plants, and weather.

At the abandoned Jewish cemetery in Douglas some graves will be nameless. Some dates missing. Some will have bird shit on their headstones. A large yucca will be growing out of a family tomb. Several graves will show the burial of a father and son, no mothers. A man, who lives next to the cemetery, will join us, and tell us how groups visit and then never come back. He is a welder. "I weld everything except broken hearts," he will say. In his shop he will show us a car turned into a grill with a skull on the engine hood.

Douglas, once a wealthy mining town with a smelter,

is one of the many border towns in the southwest dying slowly from border patrol and private prison economies. At the cemetery's entrance there will be a small inscription dedicated to the Jewish pioneers of Cochise County. I will wonder how quickly the Jewish diaspora adopted settler-colonial language in order to thrive out west. One concern raised by the small group will be the desecration of the graves. I don't know if it's the heat that confuses me, but I will be unable to remember why people desecrate. I also will not be able to recall why maintenance of graves is important. Later, in the wash of the rain, with the creosote's oils swarming freely, I will return to clarity. This is what one must do: caretake and charge, hadn't I said so many times? And yet, my own stance will seem entirely weather dependent these days. The severe conditions of the desert crack not only its own soil but also the firmament on which I have built myself. In these small abysses anything can become plausible. Opinions evaporate, as does the water in ceramic planters. The border wall behind the cemetery, rusty brown, will one day be subsumed by the same corrosion, the same generous grip. The Jewish pioneers are dead. Their graves lie abandoned.

Anastasia takes care of land, animals, stories, and occasionally dead remains. When she cleaned out the house upon moving there, she found ancient ritual tools and human bones.

"Skull parts, to be exact."

When I asked her during our visit to her homestead if she feels haunted out here, she shrugged her shoulders. "I am not ever comfortable. I always have to actively negotiate my comfort zone. But this place is, on the outside, what I am like on the inside. It's not necessarily great; it's just what it is. It often feels like I am clanging around in my own head. Let's clean this out, and this got out of control, and here is this weird dog. There are not that many layers of distraction. The human-constructed environments that we create in urban areas are all about distractions. These perceptions coming at you, peeled off like an onion when I came here. For some people that process is horrifying. There is a stripping-down process that happens. All these rules. I can't smell this way. I am going to clothe myself accordingly, not spend any time with myself naked. Sometimes life feels like a race towards death, and it takes a toll. You miss out on a lot of things. For example, what the sun feels like on your skin. Everything I do here takes longer, but I am not wasting any time. I am earning back health. One thing I have become out here is an excellent economist. I am teaching myself how to make cheese, keeping up with animals. I did pay a price. If things start coming apart, people will have to figure out the economics of everything, their own selves, their own capabilities."

At night, next to her cheese fridges, I dreamt of a large bird landing on my shoulder and of the skulls below the house. The cranes would not be at the waterhole the next morning. Instead we slid across a mud road, ate more cheese with heavier bread, added fermented vegetables to the plate. At noon Anastasia showed me the surrounding land. "We don't have a river to gauge the loss. It's all groundwater." She pointed out the rapid desertification. "The wind erosion is very bad. That's a real battle, keeping soil in place, keeping this bare, fragile ground covered."

I do not know what will happen to the cemetery. Anastasia has some ideas, another project she may take on. Why I cannot say. When we had visited her homestead, I scribbled down notes and listened to her recent discoveries: *Erich Fromm's theory on traumatic narcissism. The history of nobility. Solar farming. Goat diseases. Moving across the truth that is already here, already wielding exile, while her cat fell asleep in the frying pan.*

After our visit to Douglas and its Jewish cemetery, the monsoons will unleash. Clouds will have built throughout the day. I will think about how life here came forward in a wind, a magical spurn. To say, "I lived in the desert." The winds will grow both from below and above, fanged and in bitterroot. Clouds almost touch the ground. Tensions ingested throughout the day will now bolt through the air in the form of lightening. Screams will echo through the neighborhood as soon as the first raindrops fall.

Until the rains begin, stray animals, birds, and plants seem to be on the verge of disappearance. Only the palm trees, which I will notice more, shake boldly in the breeze. A black widow will appear on the cat carrier, which we take to Goodwill. The cicadas will rise from below and into the center, through the bones of the tree.

In the dried-out riverbed of the Santa Cruz River the ground will swell from below, caverns of water that bubble with the onset of heavier rainfall. Sewer pipes will gush through fences, overwhelming the pedestrian path. Frogs will sing from the banks, gurgling in homage. The torrents of water will bring relief. We will run through puddles and wonder how we will die, by lightning, snakebite, or in a flash flood.

Ana Mendieta once asked: "Do you fear the functionaries or the real spirit of the continent?"

Towards the final days of the monsoons we will pack up our house. We will move from the desert to water. To another border. North. Yogila, the underworld cat, will watch us carry boxes to the car. She will come inside, briefly, for some milk, and then take shade underneath the salt cedar, not let anyone touch her. We will prolong our departure. Find final surfaces to clean, watch Yogila hide in the shed. The car will be parked next to the house, close to the nameless bush where our cat died. We will light a candle on her grave, below the mesquite tree. The garden, which until the monsoons began appeared utterly dead, will re-emerge with budding blossoms. When we finally open the car doors and say "goodbye," Yogila will emerge from some corner of the shed. For a moment I will wonder if she has changed her mind and come north with us. Right before reaching the car, she will veer off and disappear into the nameless bush from where our cat had uttered her last three screams. We will wait. But Yogila will not come back out again.

ORACLE ROAD

Driving north out of Tucson on Oracle Road, you eventually pass the town of Florence, much smaller than the Renaissance city in Italy, and seamed with prisons and detention centers. The same route that those "streamlined" have to travel until they arrive at Florence's flourishing detention economy, staying for thirty, sixty, and up to one-hundred eighty days. Abutting the barbed wire of one detention center is the former POW camp, now a retirement home. Nothing but ponds, green grass. Golf carts harmlessly zoom along small lanes and miniature parking lots. South of there, another road, same asphalt, from which a hidden and yet rather sumptuous Greek Orthodox monastery can be visited. The monastery was founded in 1995, after the elder Ephraim from Mt. Athos, Greece, had a vision, which may or may not have involved seeing the land (cheap at the time), its rugged desert monastic potential, and two underground wells (later to be found and used for drinking water as well as a promotional symbol that illustrates the depth of the vision of the elder).

Within the walls of the monastery there are gardens, both Greek and tropical, Mediterranean and desert native. Visitors are instructed to walk in a particular sequence. The saints live on the walls in gilded frames. A woman, who is angry at the amount of skin visitors show, will greet us. She will hand us pins to close the slits in our dresses, long shirts to cover wrists, a shawl to properly cover our earlobes. At arrival drowsiness will set in. We will shuffle between the olive gardens from chapel to chapel, from the saint known as the "myrrh-gusher" to the saint most revered. We will shuffle in slow and deliberate movements, quietly and with our senses piqued. I will continue to wonder about human existence as one long chain of ceremonies. Ceremonies of punishment and ceremonies of reverence. The Indigenous scholar and midwife, Patrisia Gonzales, had once said to me that ceremony requires a rooting in all the necessary relationships, otherwise the ceremony becomes a performance, an appropriation of ancient cultural knowledge. "Why does a ceremony produce something extraordinary? Academics theorize around performance and the search for meaning but for many native peoples it's not just a performance or the making of meaning, these actions actually have a power and the power comes from parts of the world that we can't explain. They are invisible until the right moment emerges."

The shuffling will promote a kind of agitation from which everything will need to be suddenly contemplated: the courthouse in Tucson, where the previous week I had watched the "ceremony" of detaining between fifty and sixty people through the fast-track system known as "Operation Streamline." Those men and one woman also shuffled, but within the actual constraint of chains. They sat on benches, watching and watched, listening to the judge who did not listen.

And though the protocol maintained an automatism, the judge was confused, mixed up one man's name with one who turned out not to be the man in question. Later another man, whose first language was not Spanish and whose native language did not match the languages spoken by court interpreters in the room, was dismissed. So, despite the ceremony's attempted rigorousness, a slight air of the unexpected and impalpable moved through the courtroom that Monday.

Ideas don't scare me, but their bodies, gravities, and actions do. The monastic gardens will bloom like hallucinations. We will rest and watch a water fountain with four lion heads spewing infinite streams. Thoughts such as these will pass by: *Are we monotone, restless, spiteful and the woods and trees and light corridors of this planet are not? Have we descended like an alien force on a beatific countenance only to become its ultimate poison?* Inside one of the chapels, light will play with walls. It will be quiet. I will be alone for a brief moment, in front of a large altar. A sheet of memory will peel off. I will sit in one of the wooden chairs and focus on the saints whose names I don't know. Another thought will pass: *You will not always be able to do this.* Then an image of myself, a smear, will pull through the air. A portrait against a green background and several doubling heads slowly dissipating.

Later, when we will stop by the gift shop, sweaty and confused over whether to buy honey or olive oil or nothing at all, I will watch the gatekeeper woman scold an elderly couple that took off their shawls and layers too early. "Just because this is a commercial space, we are still in the boundaries of the monastery," the gatekeeper will admonish. Robert will storm out of the bookstore enraged. A book he opened talked of AIDS as God's punishment for homosexuality. Meanwhile, the angry woman will tell us how to use the olive oil: "It is best with some salt, pepper and oregano. Dip the bread into it. It's good like that."

I will remember visiting the detention center in Florence the previous year, also in spring. I was assisting a delegation from the Midwest who wanted to learn more about organizations and conditions in the borderlands. It was day three of the delegation and about one hundred degrees outside. We were split into groups as we entered the detention center. Two others and I sat at an oval table across from a man from El Salvador. On the table: red-colored plastic baskets with some paper and unsharpened pencils. Guards and detention personnel surrounded us. The man, a priest from El Salvador, used the visiting hour to speak of God and God's grace. His former self, a politician, he told us, was saved when he tried and failed to cross into the US. He told us that his detention was helping him hone his true vocation as a priest. I tried to imagine the priest sitting in the courtroom that precedes detention, in chains and among up to seventy other men and women in a windowless room in Tucson's federal court. Those apprehended in the desert, or at so-called non-designated ports of entry, are moved through the ad hoc system without a proper hearing. A rehearsed ritual, in which both sides agree to a script (usually relayed by one of the court-appointed lawyers right before the hearing) that sees migrants plead guilty to the charges in order for the felony offence to be reduced to a petty offence.

How do you plead to the charge of illegal entry?
Culpable.

Do you understand the rights you are giving up, the consequences of pleading guilty, and the terms of your written agreement?
Si.

Are you pleading guilty voluntarily and of your own free will?
Si.

You may be excused, good luck!

During the visit I tried to imagine the man as a powerful politician in El Salvador, then back to this windowless room, his solemn face in front of me, detained and inspired. The trajectory back and forth crumbled. I could not take notes. When our time was up, guards collected the plastic baskets with pencils and loose papers. He asked if we could write a recommendation to the judge. His hearing was coming up in a few weeks.

On our drive back from the detention center, in an air-conditioned van, one of the delegates, a pastor, was pulling at his hair. What began as water drops in the desert—after which he reflected, "It concerned me that people would have to just lay down and sleep there, not knowing where their next drink of water will come from"—had now turned even more sinister. The pastor moaned in his seat. He wrung his hands. Sweat was running down his temples. He refused the sandwich someone offered him. Then, suddenly, shouted in a loud voice, a thundering voice, across the van, "Why are all plants thorned out here?" We were speeding down Oracle Road. A red snake crossed the asphalt. Nobody seemed to see it cross and disappear into purple lupine and claret-colored penstemon.

Nicole Torres writes of the border as an "elaborate ceremonial practice of social distinction focused on citizenship and belonging." The order of the day is the order of the day. And yet, something rustles from the bushes. A mistake occurs. An unexpected death or birth. A new language suddenly fills the room for which there is no interpreter. A stranger approaches the retirement home and asks about its former life as a POW camp. The veil drops, uncovering the shoulder briefly. Does the light-filled chapel exist in separation from the angry woman who prepares visitors for entry? Can a detention center become a site of awakening to a fleeing politician? These questions came from nowhere. No, they came from somewhere, perhaps Greece, perhaps God, perhaps the hormonal ground. And any border also a place where ceremonies draw up the unseen worlds, resting not resting, to unhinge the patterns of our confinements.

STATELESS

There is the first world, the poor world, meaning it is where everything actually happens. The second world, much later much farther, is the rich world where one can reflect on what has happened, shape it again like beeswax between one's pungent hands. The first world is where one lost one's virginity to masked horsemen with wooden swords and waited by a large window to be called or forgotten. It is where the smallness yearned to grow into a reef with living corals. Latent and dusty, one had only a few possessions. One was very beautiful then and that was, for a long time, one's only fare. In exchange one received a certain attention, stories and gifts. And even though one's own stories were haggard and ineffective, one understood that this might be a bridge to another place. That a story could make the sea become a vision or a garment or a garden. They were lubricant to another space and that one, the next, could become a pause from the ongoingness of the first. The first world is forever in one's skin. It runs deep, like ground water. But one can only fully wake to it if removed. It's as if it is seamless and lapping, seamless and furtive without the distance given from the quiet days of the later world, the waiting world, the inconceivable one.

"The term 'border' often carries negative connotations," the man of history explains to me in his large office which overlooks the eastern edge of the river. Across lies the German embankment, the terrace of the Border Café, where I had a coffee an hour ago. Below, the Archive of Human Destinies, where I read with the dead.

"In Poland that is different," he adds. "The Poles experienced statelessnes in the nineteenth and twentieth century while Europe was at the height of its nationalist developments. In exactly this time period, from the farmer's movement to the right to vote, from industrialization to the emancipation of women, Poland went through these changes three times. Russian, Prussian, and Austrian. In 1918 the state of Poland had to unify these disparate experiences. Or, in other words, Poland had to find the golden thread toward becoming an autonomous state, and to this end borders are necessary. The removal of borders based on the historical experiences of Poland would not be widely accepted. The idea that over our heads lies the roof of Europe is a very foreign concept in this country."

Back in Berlin, once divided into two breast pockets, leaves talk to the rain. It seems as if everything here is calling. Sleepless for days and therefore dumbstruck, I can't seem to remember what my decisions were based on, what constituted their weight or their ease. From the window I can see the street and streetlight, the wall of the house, another window. The loss of homeland also marks the beginning of a new space into which aspects of the old are carried, and most of the world came into consciousness by shafting in and out of beings. Aeneas and the Trojans brought their gods to Rome and with it the remote East was implemented into the imperial cradle of Western heritage. Similarly, the Bible is a document affected by the textual analysis of the three main strands of Western religion. Jews used commentary (Midrash), Christians the supplementary (New Testament), and Islam the palimpsest (Revelations). Yiddish became a composite language, part High German, part Slavic, part Hebraic, for nomadic reasons. Nationless, with no fixed rules of grammar, it was for a long time dismissed as a "maiden tongue."

I imagine taking this country, cutting it out of my body, drowning it in the sea. What would it be like in here? Would it precede absence or nostalgia, a primordial crime? Instead, I buy a light bulb that will last one thousand hours and listen to Saskia Sassen speak to a half-empty room. "The Guantanamo hunger strike was inspired by the IRA hunger strike. In other words," she adds, "meaning circulates."

And I this raven with a piece of hot coal in my beak.

DIGLOSSIA

As I bike through Berlin the words "exile," "flight," and "migration" are everywhere. During the poetry festival, Ghayath Almadhoun, a Syrian-Palestinian poet, reads "The Capital." The poem is displayed in several languages. The hangover from several theoretical presentations prior has been broken. "And why do we decide to be in exile?" the poet asks, before answering his own question. "It makes for the deepest literature. And yet, I must agree with Hannah Arendt, we, the Syrian refugees, did not commit an act or expressed a political opinion that forced us to seek refuge. We are ordinary civilians. I love this woman, Hannah Arendt, very much. . . ."

I had first read Arendt as an adolescent. Her enormous dexterity was both inspiring and intimidating, which further cemented my conception of myself as an essentially limited thinker. I was interested, beyond my own personal conundrum, in her precision toward language, her impeccable German even through many years of living in exile, her natural distaste for ambition ("ambition was considered the most inferior character trait in my childhood home") and yet her carefree acknowledgement of her own brilliance. Later, I watched grainy interviews with her entranced by her acerbic tone, the dry yet incisive analysis of the Holocaust, her Jewish upbringing, and exile. In one of her later appearances, she described her first return to Germany in 1949, as a kind of *anagnosis* a total recognition of what had happened, before moving on to the topic of the sudden loss of the mother tongue suffered by many of her contemporaries in exile. "What follows this loss is a language which chases clichés, because it has been cut off from its original productivity." I still cannot fully fathom the meaning of "original productivity," but have felt the loss of language, the replacement, the layering of a new semantic system on top of the old, in my own body. My first language, German, lying awkwardly between jaws, choked on or paused, half formulated and moldy.

The panel has dispersed and people wait for the rains to calm, drink coffee, and eat *Torte*. I leave the festival and ride my bike through the Tiergarten. The "animal garden" is where I spent the first months of my life as a newborn. It is the greenest memory I have. Steam rises from the asphalt, and as I begin my transversal back into the German language, the word "puddle" remains momentarily nameless. But through the steam and green wilderness of my first park, fragments of the poem return and rise from the nameless puddle. I turn to them and listen, relinquish the desire to become something relatable.

AUGURY

I cross several more puddles before suddenly remembering the word again, *Pfütze,* as my tires divide its dancing edges. The edges transport me to the spring of 2009, also puddle filled. I had spent a morning in front of the Office of Immigration Services on Tooley Street in London. It was, as so often, a foggy and distant morning. I had time and didn't know why I had come. Or at least my plan was vague, a little sheepish. I wanted to talk to someone who was making an asylum claim or whose claim had been rejected. I wanted to meet people who had recently arrived here. In my backpack I had a list of questions, crossing Europe with a naïve pragmatism, never knowing my way but always getting there eventually. London was packed. There was not a spot of space with a nothing in it. Children in the tight grip of their mothers' hands passed, looking shyly from below their hats. Sometimes I smiled first, sometimes they did. I watched families hush up the steps. They entered through glass doors, and, I imagined, metal detectors before crossing the threshold, surrounded by bodies of Home Office officials. I felt I had no business entering and no business watching these people enter. Even less noble seemed my objective to ask them to sit down with me and answer further questions. Why would they be interested in telling their complex story to yet another stranger?

Shortly after feeling at the point of excessive uselessness, a man hurried down the steps. He was well dressed, looked around then approached me. We were, in fact, walking towards each other. He slowed down his pace, and we met halfway between the bottom of the stairs and the sidewalk. I explained myself hurriedly, and asked if he wanted some tea. He agreed. We began to walk down Tooley Street. He spoke English well and was comfortable with my proposal, even when I asked if I could record our conversation.

The only thing I can do is write, now as then. Challenge usually begins with a mood. A nun was running down the street and I remember thinking that it was a bad omen. That was before I knew that the interpretation of omens belongs to the craft of augury, originally a practice from ancient Rome, reading the flight of birds (*aves*). When the individual, known as the augur, interpreted these signs it was referred to as "taking the auspices." "Augur" and "auspices" are from the Latin *auspicium* and *auspex*, literally "one who looks at birds." Depending upon the birds, the auspices from the gods could be favorable or unfavorable (*auspicious* or *inauspicious*). Sometimes bribed or politically motivated augurs would fabricate unfavorable auspices in order to delay certain state functions, such as elections.

We sat down in a crowded café. He began to tell me his story. Began to tell me how he had left Iran, how he could not go back, how he was unable to procure papers, and today he had received his third and last rejection of his asylum claim. He said he was now officially "illegal" in this country. I was going to take a train back to Brussels the next morning, and I thought briefly about whether I should offer him my ticket. But being undocumented in Brussels or in London makes little difference. He said he had some friends here and would live on their couches until he could get a lawyer. It occurred to me that he might have money, that he might be independently wealthy. We drank tea. I did not take notes, relying on my recording device.

Outside of the café moments and people passed without consequence. His political activity, which was never specified, forced him to leave, first on a student visa and later as one of many seeking humanitarian protection. I had learned that the language of the Geneva Convention around humanitarian protection was both broad and impenetrable. To prove the likelihood of persecution upon return to their home country, claimants had to either provide documentary evidence or have a good lawyer present their future corpse convincingly to the courts.

He could have been a fellow student or a friend. He said he might go to Amsterdam, Stockholm, or Switzerland. Iran? No, never. He could marry. I lingered on this thought while sipping my lukewarm tea. Shortly after we shook hands. I left before him, Tooley filling with rush-hour humans.

That night I had some wonderful Middle Eastern food with my friends, who let me sleep in their closet recently rebranded as bedroom. The bedroom did not have any windows. The heaters were broken but jumped on for an hour, usually just before dawn, and we all woke soaked. The next morning I got on several buses and was dropped off at St. Pancras Station, where I stepped onto the Eurostar train, traveling below sea level then coming up for air at Calais. Many months later, I would find myself stuck in this train below sea level for two hours due to repairs after a fire had swept through the tunnel. When the Eurostar flew across northern France and into Belgium, the dogs came sniffing through the coaches.

Over the course of that year I spoke with asylum seekers, refugees, undocumented migrants, and stateless people. The conversations began with distances, their own language to mine, their country of origin to their country of refuge, crossing the Sahara Desert, or the growing void between what happened and how they remembered it happening. At the center lingered the experience of their current legal status and the various interview techniques immigration officials had employed to elicit their pasts, techniques mostly aimed at detecting inconsistencies and falsehood in their narratives.

When I returned home from these conversations to my desk, silences enveloped the room. Within these silences I began to notice myself walking along the rims of coasts, of land, where histories and descriptions continue to shape a failure towards the ultimate mystery of the other, our shared signal drifting beyond the edge, far out at sea.

Several years later, I visited an exhibition in Marseille, mother of all port cities, and at the lapping waters of the Mediterranean Sea. The exhibit was dedicated to the history and culture of Mediterranean civilizations. It moved swiftly across time, from Babylonian ramparts and palaces to the establishment of maritime trade routes. A neon sign flashed *The Weeping Wall Inside Us All*. The day before a taxi driver told me that Mary Magdalene had arrived on these shores by boat, a Palestinian refugee. "She not only miraculously survived the Mediterranean, she was later sanctified," he exclaimed. The exhibition ranged from the elusive dream the blue waters had inspired in artists and writers to the rivalry between Europe and the Ottoman Empire, Napoleon's expedition to Egypt and Saint Simon's vision of a symbiosis between east and west. Marseille, recently honored as European Capital of Culture city, strategically located the museum, a large concrete cuboid by the water with small mosaic openings in its façade, between the new and old port. The museum faced south towards the water, which at a certain point reaches Africa, the Maghreb. Six-hundred sixty million euro were invested into the "unfinished" city. A renovated train station, a new national museum, a port and former tobacco factory turned cultural center are some of the ventures *la bonne mère*, patron mother of Marseille, is now protecting alongside her traditional role as watchful eye over the many seafaring children that arrived and continue to arrive here.

From the museum you could look out to the sea of pain, the sea of contact, the sea cemetery and its cruise ships, fishing boats, and dancing nets of sunlight. Along its rim small alleys, light blue window shutters. All unrecorded conversations out there. All surviving objects in here. That summer I read a newspaper article in which the mayor of Lampedusa wept at the shores where over three hundred people drowned, after their frail barque caught fire. She cried out amidst her official press statement, "All these bodies are speaking."

Omens no one dares to read.

As I exit the Tiergarten, the rain and mist lifting from puddles and verdant patches of grass, his voice or the memory of his voice reaches me, so many years after walking down Tooley Street together.
"Do you know the actual meaning of *abraq ad habra*?"
"No."
"It means, I will create as I speak."

MOONSCAPES

Not far from the Tiergarten, in the same room in which Saskia Sassen spoke of circulating meanings, the writer Mariam Ghani talks about "moonscapes," looted archeological sites in the war theaters of Iraq and Afghanistan. "Have you seen the Bactrian princesses?" she wonders. "They are composite stone figures, assembled from various separate pieces, made of dark green chlorite or steatite with white limestone, usually from Afghanistan, Uzbekistan, Turkmenistan, and for a while part of a permanent exhibition at Documenta. Migratory objects can still find free ports these days and antiquities change hands, travel *sub rosa*, in exchange for arms. We could always consider archeological sites the scene of a crime. What we hear are conversations and images about Palmyra, the ruins, never Palmyra, the city." It is quiet. Her "we" different from the "we" present in the room. She stares at the audience, then asks in rapid succession three questions:

"How distant does the past have to be for it to become safe for cultural consumption?"

"How much will we be asked to forget to become accepted members of this census community?"

"And who" [*pauses*] "is the thief?"

TRAINSTATION

This summer the rainiest in years. It is August the 11th. It will be my last time taking the train to the archive and back to the city. When I asked the director what motivated him to create an archive of life stories, he laughed, then said that there are often secret motivations, those we never fully understand, that bring an idea to life. Why we do what we do, why we do what we do when we do it, why we do what we do the way we do it.

I run across the bridge, past the empty control houses, women selling asparagus. The river arms meet below the bridge, the way all our hands touch below the table, in the lowest places. There is this long steep hill to the train station against which I have lost many times. I am sure it will be the same today and blisters will form on both feet. I am sure it will happen just as it has before, arriving the moment the train departs, unless something else is moved too, made late, turned around.

At the train station lean bodies salute. I watch a woman who takes her country, her skin— a kind of suitcase— and looks at her watch.

"Could it be that time is too narrow for all events? Could it happen that all the seats within time might have been sold? Worried, we run along the train of events, preparing ourselves for the journey."

A train with only three compartments comes to a halt. "It is going nowhere," the woman with the watch says. "There is another one arriving in a few minutes on the adjacent platform that will pass through Berlin. It will not wait. Hurry!"

Back at Berlin Ostbahnhof, where I get off, I come across an exhibit titled *WARonWALL*, which shows twenty-two images of destroyed Syrian cities and wounded children on a preserved remainder of the Berlin wall. The wall is close to the train station and a popular tourist attraction with grassy slopes. The images show children with amputated limbs, rubble, and razed neighborhoods. Next to the pictures: stories about how these children lost their limbs, usually from shelling and shrapnel. What time of day it was, how they were treated or failed to get treated. Their bodies are as tall as the wall. Tourists pass half-struck. Their mouths tight, eyes squinted. Green grass follows at the bottom of the images, below the wall's ruins, an unnatural extension of gray stones. It appears that the images are a panoptical view into the past, a former iteration of the ground on which people sunbathe and picnic. Occasionally, also, the feeling that this might be the future, a kind of double vision of rubble and grass, of amputation and walking, those who suffer towering in large posters over those who are not wounded or missing limbs.

GROUNDSWELL

The Polish word *granica,* meaning little twig, is the root for the German word *Grenze.* Slavonic farmers used to protect their fields with thorny twigs, which was perceived by Germanic tribes as an act of segregation.

The chestnut tree outside of the house lost a large branch overnight, which now obstructs the courtyard.

I dream of water corpses, a particularly deformed and ghoulish version of the corpse. We try to locate these bodies to avoid that they poison the groundwater. We wade through canals. We, the people, who are aware that these corpses exist in the first place. After a long time of unsuccessful searching I return to the house. In the kitchen a faucet is behaving oddly. Water begins to bubble from the pipes. I realize that the corpses have arrived and are pushing the water upward. They are trying to talk, making their way through the sink system. I do not want to see the dead bursting through the faucet and so I decide to wake.

The presentation "Groundswell," which I must give at the end of my stay to students at Viadrina University, fails. I am somewhat of a keynote speaker, but what I will speak about has nothing to do with marginalized languages or quantitative research methods. There is complete silence, icy quiet in the room. I already know what will happen and therefore simply read my notes:

The border as text itself . . . The framework a chorographic atlas . . . originally comprised of a mixture of folklore, natural history, travel writings, hearsay, historical events, analysis of collected and or described items, visualization, oral testimony, the discursive, the factual as well as the fictional . . . to study a specific region or landscape . . . To etch out a cultural commons that the geopolitical space rejects . . .

When I look up I see Nina in the audience. At the end of my talk nobody has any questions, except for an elderly professor who does not really ask but rather reproaches me. He struggles to understand my methodology, my system. Before he finishes his lengthy comment, Nina walks up to me and grabs my hand, pulls me gently towards the door. I wave to everyone before leaving the room. Once outside, we drive to her favorite lake, one of the many that surround Berlin. It is late summer and my return is coming to an end. We spread a blanket on the grass and she begins to undress. I want to write while she goes for a swim in the lake. I imagine a camera next to me filming her body's immersion. I will wait on the shore as she crosses the deft surface. Just like the camera, I will watch. We can perform consciousness; at times explain at times stutter. Sometimes no language at all. First she will disappear and then she will reappear. I want to write about how we ebb and flow, how her sacrifices return a piece of life to me. My absences become boxes with breath for her next turning. We interlock arms and dance a May dance until the grass catches us. Living proof of our waning, our branching. Maybe none of this will happen and instead she will drown and I will swim after her.

CROSSINGS

What do we take into the future?

***

At the entrance I read the words "Verboten/Forbidden" in old German typography. The room is air conditioned, but the air is thick with dust and I am the only person moving through these rooms. The exhibit is an excerpt from the Austellung 'Entartete Kunst' curated by the Nazis and first shown in Munich in 1937 with the singular goal "to humiliate and desecrate" art and artists who the Nazis deemed "degenerate." It featured work by Käthe Kollwitz, Paul Klee, Marc Chagall, Pablo Picasso, Max Ernst, and Oskar Kokoschka among others.

The "Verboten/Forbidden" exhibit, shown in a North American town close to the Mexican border, is empty. Its presence a sign from a sunken world and similar to the seawater that once roiled here, these absences pierce the walls with peculiar shapes, phantoms, heat pearls. A gargle of time and drifts.

The original Austellung 'Entartete Kunst' opened in July with around 16,000 works on display and traveled to twelve other German and Austrian cities through November 1937. Paintings were sloppily hung, ideally in dilapidated frames, with graffiti that insulted the work. The large numbers of visitors may have been due to the exhibit's blunt acknowledgement of what is "forbidden," an opportunity to trespass in public and with state support. It may have resulted from the exceptional art on display. Or simply proving the obvious: civic life goes on, performs in accordance with and close proximity to the humiliation of others.

The collection, which displayed "weakness of character, mental disease and racial impurity" never conclusively defined the term "degenerate," but often made reference to the minds of the insane or a work's Jewish characteristics. It is hard to know how this must have felt to the artists in question. Ernst Ludwig Kirchner committed suicide shortly after the exhibit opened. Many emigrated and never returned. Some of the works, such as Christian Rohlfs's paintings, were put on a canvass and covered with the contents of various tubes of paint, vigorously smeared, and then placed in a frame. The instructions go beyond the desire to censor or decry certain aesthetic inclinations and read at times as a perverted impulse to be part of the "degeneration" of the work itself, add layers and signatures to its existence. I imagine the men who carried out these instructions. Did they feel impassioned destroying someone else's work? Inspired? Did they begin to make sketches in the dark? Did they have any thoughts at all? Human hands lifting, carrying away, hitting nails into walls.

It remains inconclusive as to why the Nazis lavished so much attention onto what was, then, largely considered marginal art. After the Austellung 'Entartete Kunst' concluded its "tour," many of the works were destroyed or auctioned off to, in Goebbels words, "at least make some money of this garbage."

In this heat mirror the art appears strangely out of place, and yet its language familiar. These costumes of economic takeover, nationalism, and deprivation draped over other bodies.

***

When I drove to the border a few weeks earlier, the black-bordered patch butterfly cast a shadow over dry soil. I was accompanied by a former border patrol agent turned writer. We wove through Organ Pipe Cactus National Monument, before stopping close to a border fence. When we approached the fence, a border patrol vehicle appeared. The two men conversed with in a cordial tone and then explained to me that we set off a sensor. We stared at a faint print in the sand.

"This is our footprint. You can see the design from the sole of the shoe. This has recently been dragged. You see how smooth it is? If I had done this an hour ago and drove back and saw our footprints, I would get out of my car and see how far I could follow the sign."

While we drove toward the entry point at Sonoita and ate our snacks, the writer reflected on his time in the border patrol, the largest federal law-enforcement agency in the US, in shifting terms: "I never outwardly violated my own moral code, but later, when thinking about the repercussions of the work and looking back at being a participant of an inherently violent structure, I began to feel some culpability."

He switched between reproach and vivid memory, recounting his daily routine:

"You are in your car, a sensor goes off, you think, cool, I am going to go and check it out and either you know how to work the sensor or you can call another senior agent who will tell you: 'Go and park your car at mile marker four, then skirt those foothills until you get to the wash and if the group that hit that sensor is on that trail, you should be able to jump them at that point.' You go do it, and half the time nothing comes down the trail, maybe an animal set off the sensor, or wind. You are walking alone, and so you will let people know what you are doing, but your nearest backup might be thirty minutes away, and a lot of times I would be out there by myself, at night. You have this whole background of experience that has led you to believe that you are capable to enter the situation. You have a long arm and your radio; you have every advantage over the situation, other than the fact that you may be completely outnumbered which is usually the case. If a group comes down the trail, you jump out of the bushes and scare the bejesus out of everyone. You do everything in your power to establish control over the situation; you project that you are a big scary agent to not mess with. I speak fluent Spanish, which was a big advantage. Your primary concern is to do all the things you've been trained to do to bring this group in. Walk these people out to the road in single file, use these little cloth handcuffs. You also make them take their shoelaces out of their shoes, so when they try to run, their shoes are just going to fly off. You transport them back to the station. You enter them into the system and file their preliminary paperwork for deportation or voluntary return to Mexico."

I could never quite tell how his moral code and the private and gradual sense of culpability interacted as he patrolled the landscape. When I mentioned Hannah Arendt's "banality of evil" he nodded his head. "Yes, that makes perfect sense," he said.

***

Hannah Arendt wrote "We Refugees" in the early 1940s while in exile, laying out a fundamental and brilliant analysis of the modern German-Jewish condition, a protracted migratory identity that then threatened statehood and nationalism. The eternal and yet failed attempts of Jews to assimilate ("You can hardly realize how serious we were about it") went beyond adjusting to the country they were born into and to the people whose language they happened to speak ("We adjust in principle to everything and everybody"). Despite 150 years of Jewry proving their non-Jewishness, they "succeeded in remaining Jews all the same." Arendt equates the Jew to the refugee, not protected by citizenship and whose stateless identity bears an ongoing political threat. "If we should start telling the truth that we are nothing but Jews, it would mean that we expose ourselves to the fate of human beings who, unprotected by any specific law or political convention, are nothing but human beings. I can hardly imagine an attitude more dangerous, since we actually live in a world in which human beings as such have ceased to exist for quite a while; since society has discovered discrimination as the great social weapon by which one may kill men without bloodshed; since passports or birth certificates, and sometimes even income tax receipts, are no longer formal papers but matters of social distinction."

***

When we drove away from the border and through the rocky national park, seamed with organ pipe cacti, stems rising vertically from a single short trunk just above ground level, the writer exclaimed: "The desert is so beautiful!" He pointed to the organ pipe: "This is the only place in this country where the organ pipe can grow and survive. It's this tiny zone that reaches into the US. Once you cross the border, they are everywhere."

Several months later, I drove the same route with Maegan, a student researcher at the Jewish History Museum and member of the Tohono O'odham nation. The landscape this time wove another narrative. She pointed to the mountain, now known as Kitt Peak, a national observatory for "nighttime astronomy" run by the National Science Foundation. The sacred mountain was lost, in Maegan's words, because of illegible documents, dense jargons, and white lawyers. "Now the observatory is part of our culture, part of our history, just like the border patrol. They have started to dip their heels into our communities. You see them at events. They hand out flyers and offer free activities. Baton tosses!" She then recounted how she once almost lost control of her vehicle as she was overtaken by border patrol during a high-speed chase. "I saw this metal scrap, like a snake, that moves fast with shiny skin across the asphalt. I made it off the road just in time, but I was so distracted by these spikes. Spikes flung across the road to puncture tires."

Maegan's family has lived close to the border for generations. During her early childhood, the border was just a barbed wire fence, where her family would collect woodchips and kindling. "A wound has living entities around it, always processing how to fix itself, correct and coagulate."

***

I will remember the drive again, the organ pipe and heat, many months later during winter temperatures in the far north, crossing from Canada back into the US. Robert and I will be pulled out of the lane for inspections. We will be handed an orange slip of paper, directed to park our car and go into the building adjacent to the checkpoint. The building will look quiet and sleepy, but once we enter through the glass doors a long queue reminiscent of airport TSA check lines will present itself. There will be about forty people lined up and they will all, except for us and two longhaired white dudes, be of Middle Eastern, Asian, or African descent.

While waiting in line, carefully reading the situation and its possible outcomes, I will feel a rising anxiety, my own and that of others in the room, take hold. The feeling subtle; on the outside everyone follows protocol, a routine, a waste of time. However, as the minutes pass, as the men enter and exit side rooms, as the agents undergo a shift change, as the empty plant pot is thrown into a large garbage bin, as the glass porcelain display grows increasingly distasteful, as people make their way from one end of the room to the other to pay the fines they are told they owe, as the sound of keys handed over the desk grows shrill, as the agents banter in their own code language, as a blonde female agent hurts her thumb and is instantly surrounded by four male agents protectively investigating her finger, as an older agent walks past the line smiling, I will feel the mysterious white space grow thick and convulsive. The lost minutes that do not get noted in historical accounts, the feeling of uncertainty, humiliation, and anger mounting in one's throat, like the glowing specter of a sunrise in late winter. A searing sensation of a mysterious shame will spread, as it does when told to take off one's hat in one's own car, to strip down in a side room, or when commanded in one's mother tongue to take out the shoelaces from one's shoes and waddle through the desert.

***

When I had crossed the threshold, back, back into the other land, I listened for the first bird that dares to sing in the morning. There at the border in the cumulative heat, a mirror appeared. One of glass shards and broken parts that form the face of an old woman. A grandmother of great insight, perhaps. Or just my own self, occupying another realm on the other side. I waited for a signal or message but the border was listless, almost lifeless. I began to doubt my presence. I was born of two people. I was born of myself. Assiduous birthing. Goodbye country that knew me when I was a grape. I began to recount my questions: Where do we end, where do we become visible? What might I offer?

On the other side, the side of gargle and drifts, there continue to be voices. "There is," as Plato said, "thirst and no one drinks according to it." The bird song is cacophonous and unruly. A sense that "underneath the concrete and underneath the towns an old ancient dreaming spirit is waiting for people to live in the right way, and when you do it you have a kind of genius underneath you that you as a person don't just possess." There is a mound that I address. A stone from your body, a comma separating your name, your longing organ, your loudest dog, broken languages rising.

NOTES

Epigraph

The epigraph is a direct quote from an interview between Saija Kaskinen and Enni, an inhabitant of the Karelian borderlands (between Russia and Finland).

— Saija Kaskinen, "If the Borders Could Tell: The Hybrid Identity of the Border in the Karelian Borderland"

page 20: Image taken by author while walking Berlin's former east-west division.

Chorography

Sebastian Münster's *Cosmographia* (1544) is the earliest German-language description of the world. The term "chorography" has been defined by Ptolemy as the study of the world's smaller parts—provinces, regions, cities, or ports. Its goal was "an impression of a part, as when one makes an image of just an ear or an eye"; and it dealt with "the qualities rather than the quantities of the things that it sets down" (Wikipedia). The term has been used for written accounts of regions extensively visited by the writer, who then combined local topographical description, summaries of historical sources, and local knowledge and stories, into a text.

I used the idea of a multivocal textual map as a starting point for the kind of place-based writing I wanted to undertake. In addition, I was curious about the many terms connected to borders, their metaphysical abstraction and absurdism. Some of these terms, as well as the notion of a glossary, I wanted to reimagine and reclaim. Over the years, I began to think of the text more as a collection of stories and voices I encountered and as part of the ground, its historical consciousness and wounding. The specific conditions of that ground, in this case borders, weave these different geographies and time frames to one another, so that the very localized and specific history begins to belong to a much wider "map." Necessarily, the routes, their threads also lead inward. The textual map, infused by voices, exists in relationship to the listener and is highly subjective.

Formation

page 8: *Another writer, who I only saw once coming through the breezeway, had written a book called* Krankheit als Weg.

Krankheit als Weg is by Thorwald Dethlefsen and Ruediger Dahlke. Dethlefsen did not live on Nollendorfstrasse, as far as I know. Another writer, whose name has escaped me, actually appeared in the breezeway. Nonetheless these figures merge in my imagination.

Parallel Time

page 10: *"But when one is burdened with contraband of supernumerary events that cannot be registered, one cannot be too fussy."*

— Bruno Schulz, *The Street of Crocodiles* (translated by Celina Wieniewska)

page 10: *"The Age of Genius,"* one of the fragments that survive from Bruno Schulz's vanished book Messiah, *evokes the necessity for parallel streams of time.*

For years, Bruno Schulz labored over a novel, referred to as "Messiah." It is unclear if the text ever fully existed and despite the staggering recovery work by Schulz biographer Jerzy Ficowski, its contents remain shrouded in mystery. Most likely the manuscript, among his many letters and paintings, were destroyed during the Shoah, though Ficowski's lifelong search implies that it may still exist somewhere. Two fragments, however, which Ficowski is certain belonged to the work were included in the 1937 collection *Sanatorium Under the Sign of the Hourglass* (translated by Celina Wieniewska), "The Book" and "The Age of Genius."

In 1941, the German Gestapo officer Felix Landau, in charge of the labor force in the Drohobycz ghetto, offered Schulz extra protections and food in exchange for several mural paintings he commissioned the Jewish artist and writer to paint. These protections did not save him or his archive. Ultimately another Gestapo officer killed Schulz after Landau executed this officer's "protégée," a Jewish dentist.

I personally had little knowledge of Ficoswki or Schulz prior to my return to Germany. Their work and lives were invoked during my many train rides from and to Frankfurt Oder, in which I spent hours talking with the German poet and translator Lothar Quinkenstein. His writings on Schulz and the Kabbala in "Bruno Schulz –ein Kabbalist der Moderne" further deepened my understanding of Schulz's work.

page 10: *In the lost manuscript,* Messiah, *childhood is understood as the primary mystic and messianic time.*

For Schulz (and different from Walter Benjamin) messianic time is the experience of an immediate and intensive awareness of the world, a particular form of perception only experienced in childhood. This realm is later difficult to access, however, can be occasionally reanimated through art and the imagination.

page 10: *"It is my longing," he wrote, "to mature toward childhood."*

In a letter to Andrzej Pleśniewicz (1936) Schulz wrote: "this kind of art, the kind that is so dear to my heart, is precisely a regression, a return to childhood. Were it possible to turn back development, achieve a second childhood by some circuitous road, once again have its fullness and immensity—that would be an incarnation of an 'age of genius,' 'messianic times' which are promised and pledged to us by all mythologies. My goal is to 'mature into childhood.' This would really be a true maturity." I changed the wording of Robertson's translation slightly, based on a German version of the sentence.

— Cited in Jerzy Ficowski's *Regions of the Great Heresy* (translated by Theodosia Robertson)

University

In 2016 I spent three months at the German-Polish border. Supported by a DAAD (German Academic Exchange Service) research grant and hosted by the Linguistics Seminar, led by Konstanze Jungbluth at Viadrina University, I spent much of that time in a kind of double existence. I was there as a writer and as a person who was longing to "come home," and also as a researcher with dubious credentials expected to present findings. In the end this double identity proved useful, led me to many forms of encounters, conversations and readings.

The following two terms framed my initial proposal:

Borderer/Grenzgaenger: "An itinerant of the in-between spaces, a goer who trains his eye on the hidden or latent geographies and does not allow him/herself to be constrained by urban borders and monolithic and statist interpretations of spaces . . . we worked towards becoming borderers ourselves (Grenzgaenger), writers and thinkers between and beyond disciplines and internal disciplination."

— Henk van Houtum, "Remapping Borders," in *A Companion to Border Studies*

Borderscapes: "The borderscape—shaped through representations of all kinds—implies borderscaping as practices through which the imagined border is established and experienced as real. Borders have not been disappearing but they are moving instead. Thus, the borderscapes concept registers the necessity to investigate borders not as taken-for-granted entities exclusively connected to the territorial limits of nation-states, but as mobile, relational and contested sites, thereby exploring alternative border imaginaries 'beyond the line.'"

— Chiara Brambilla, Jussi Laine, James W. Scott, and Gianluca Bocchi, in *Borderscaping: Imaginations and Practicies of Border Making*

Twin City

page 19: *"We share everything, even heating. Our children learn both languages and there is a bus line between the two towns. We exchange our jobs occasionally. Right now the mayors have swapped offices."*

— From an interview with Sören Bollman, who runs the Frankfurt-Slubice Cooperation Center.

White Zones

page 21: *"When something disappears in the world an empty room is created. If I enter this space, I can begin to perceive what once happened here. Warsaw's ghetto, now Muranow, did not even have ruins."*

This is my own translation of a conversation between Lothar Quinkenstein and myself in which he quotes from Ficowski's short prose piece "Die leeren Räume danach" in "Amulety i definicje" ("Amulets und Definitions," 1960).

In Quinkenstein's analysis, and in particular citing the final poem in the collection "Drohobycz 1920", the disappearance of someone from the world of the living leaves behind an empty room that is not empty but branches out into all directions. The disappeared exist in multiple spaces at once. The physical nonexistence, a kind of psychic fluid, becomes "the mole of the darkest earth of our dreams" / "gräbt als Maulwurf seine Gänge durch die Schwarzerde unserer Träume."

page 21: *In Ficowski's poem sequence "Errata," which means printing error, the poem becomes the smuggled unofficial version of history that cannot be otherwise transported.*

Errata (1980), is a collection of poems by Jerzy Ficowski in which the poem is seen as the correction of the official narrative escaping censorship. One of the poems of the collection is titled "Ringelblum Archive" (also known as the Oyneg Shabbes archive) after Emanuel Ringelblum, the Polish-Jewish social historian.

Human Destinies

The Archive of Human Destinies can be found in the basement of the Collegium Polonicum in Slubice, Poland. Original material was translated and excerpted from the MyLife project housed in the archive. I am indebted to Krzysztof Wojciechowski who provided access to the archive and gave me permission to work with the material in translation and in a creative context. I am also indebted to Karolina Stanek who helped me find biographies particularly connected to the border story of the Oder region. The original biographies were first recorded and then transcribed and edited by the archivists in collaboration with the participants; many life stories are between twenty and fifty pages long. I selected certain key images and events of these stories and then translated these into English. They are therefore shortened versions; however, my goal was to stay as faithful as possible to the chronology, tone, voice, and rhythm of the German original. In accordance with the archive's agreement all names have been changed.

Landflucht

page 52: *Bleiben will ich, wo ich nie gewesen bin.*

Bleiben will ich, wo ich nie gewesen bin. Ein Abend fuer Thomas Brasch. Von und mit Marion Brasch. In a collage work of film, text, and live reading, Marion Brasch tells the story of her dissident brother, the East German poet Thomas Brasch (1945-2001). The title of the event is taken from one of Brasch's most famous lines "Bleiben will ich, wo ich nie gewesen bin" originally published as part of the poem collection *Kargo: 32* (1977). The translation is my own.

page 55: *"Or does the return, its impossibility, signal nostalgia, longing for a different time, rather than a different place?"*

Svetlana Boym writes that the word "nostalgia" comes from two Greek roots: "νόστος, *nóstos* ("return home") and ἄλγος, *álgos* ("longing"). Boym writes, "I would define it as a longing for a home that no longer exists or has never existed. Nostalgia is a sentiment of loss and displacement, but it is also a romance with one's own phantasy."

— Svetlana Boym, *The Future of Nostalgia* (2001).

Pilgrimage

page 58: *Why is telling a story considered an act of love?*

— Kris Kraus, *Aliens and Anorexia*

Post-Transgression Syndrome

"Separation (and the existence of borders) foster(s) a certain yearning; transgressing (them) was, and in some cases, still is, a thrilling moment of experiencing what is different beyond a cultural threshold. But once borders have been crossed one can soon be faced with a paralyzing sense of saturation."

— Rüdiger Görner, "Notes on the Culture of Borders," in *Border Poetics De-limited*

Pilgrimage

page 60: *"One day earlier Benjamin would have got through without any trouble; one day later the people in Marseilles would have known that for the time being it was impossible to pass through Spain. Only on that particular day was the catastrophe possible."*

— Hannah Arendt, introduction to *Illuminations*

Excerpts of Walter Benjamin's journey to Portbou from *www. walterbenjaminportbou.com* and Michael Taussig's *Walter Benjamin's Grave* (University of Chicago Press, 2006). Most of this text is taken directly from the blog. Benjamin's notion of messianic time is also relevant to my understanding of time in *Groundswell*. "Messianic time" is explored in Benjamin's "On the Concept of History" also known as "Theses on the Philosophy of History," the assumed methodology underlying the manuscript it is said he carried in his suitcase across the Pyrenees. Messianic time contrasts the emptiness of homogenous time. To Benjamin, it is the experience of immediacy, and nonlinear connections between past, present, and future events. It is a rupture establishing continuities with subterranean histories. A revolutionary moment is a rupture of homogenous empty time and an opportunity for messianic time to enter. All life is reconciled and compressed into a single moment.

— Andy McLaverty Robinson, "Walter Benjamin: Messianism and Revolution–Theses on History," in *Ceasefire*

Oyneg Shabbes

page 64: *The night before Thanksgiving, a Wednesday, Robert will perform INTERNAL. An adaption of Leyb Goldin's "Chronicle of a Single Day" composed, buried, and exhumed in the Warsaw Ghetto.* . . .

"Chronicle of A Single Day" is an experimental and densely intertextual autobiographical story on starvation in the Warsaw ghetto in August 1941, preserved by Emanuel Ringelblum's Oyneg Shabbes underground archive.

— Leyb Goldin, *The Literature of Destruction*

Cemetery

The excursion to the Jewish cemetery, now in Poland, was possible thanks to Magda Abraham-Diefenbach whose extensive research and writing on the site can be found in *Makom Tov-der gute Ort. Juedischer Friedhof Frankfurt Oder/ Slubice* (2012)

page 73: *Ana Mendieta once asked: "Do you fear the functionaries or the real spirit of the continent?"*

— Ana Mendieta, cited in *Unseen Mendieta* by Olga Viso

Oracle Road

page 77: *I assisted a delegation from the Midwest...*
For a brief time, I worked for the Tucson based organization BorderLinks, an educational organization that leads delegations and explores the impact of US immigration policies on migrant communities in the borderlands.

page 77: *Operation Streamline*
My writing and thinking on Operation Streamline was greatly influenced by Brandon Shimoda's work: https://thenewinquiry.com/operation-streamline/

page 79: *Nicole Torres writes of the border as an "elaborate ceremonial practice of social distinction focused on citizenship and belonging."*

— Nicole I. Torres, *Walls of Indifference: Immigration and the Militarization of the US-Mexico Border*

Stateless

page 82: *Instead, I buy a light bulb that will last one thousand hours and listen to Saskia Sassen speak to a half-empty room.*

Saskia Sassen spoke to a half-empty room at the "Migratory People, Migratory Objects" symposium in Berlin in 2016.

Diglossia

I lean into various definitions here, though most specifically Diglossia as the presence of two tongues as well as its Greek origin díglōss(os) speaking two languages (from encyclopedia.com)

page 84: *What follows this loss…*

The translation is my own. Also, the order of themes is different in the original interview than I have represented here.

— Hannah Arendt in "Zur Person" interview: *https://www.youtube.com/watch?v=dsoImQfVsO4&t=43s*

Augury

Appeared as part of *Abraq Ad Habra I Will Create As I Speak* (Essay Press, 2016 www.essaypress.org/ep-58). The chapbook was a response to research I conducted as part of my master's thesis in migration studies, analyzing the role of narrative in the context of asylum claims in Britain, Belgium, and Malta. The qualitative study asked: how are private, culturally specific and traumatic personal experiences transposed into a rationalized juridical framework? I interviewed claimants, immigration lawyers, judges, expert witnesses, grassroots organizations, activists, court interpreters, and found that in the absence of physical documentation, the applicant's story often becomes a central piece of evidence in a court hearing. However, the nature of narrative—circular, nonlinear with gaps and inconsistencies, highly dependent on the person to whom the story is recounted—is usually interpreted by court officials as lacking in credibility and dismissed. The encounter explored in *Augury* was a conversation that I never transcribed and that only exists in my memory.

page 88: *"The exhibit was dedicated to the history and culture of Mediterranean civilizations."*

— "The Black and the Blue, a Mediterranean Dream," exhibit at Mucem, Marseille, 2014.

Moonscapes

Inspired by a talk given by Mariam Ghani titled "Culture Wars" and presented as part of the "Migratory People, Migratory Objects" symposium in Berlin in 2016.

Trainstation

page 93: *"The river arms meet below the bridge, the way all our hands touch below the table, in the lowest places." I am not certain, but this line might have been inspired by Bruno Schulz, who wrote: "For, under the imaginary table that separates me from my readers, don't we secretly clasp each others hands?"*

— Bruno Schulz, "The Book" in *The Street of Crocodiles* (translated by Celina Wieniewska)

page 94: *"Could it be that time is too narrow for all events?"*

— Bruno Schulz, "The Age of Genius" in *The Street of Crocodiles* (translated by Celina Wieniewska)

Groundswell

page 95: *"The Polish word* granica, *meaning little twig, is the root for the German word Grenze."*

— Rüdiger Görner, "Notes on the Culture of Borders" in *Border Poetics De-limited*

Crossings

page 98: *At the entrance I read the words "Verboten/Forbidden" in old German typography.*

— "Verboten/Forbidden," exhibit at University of Arizona Museum of Art, 2017.

page: 103: *"If we should start telling the truth..."*

— Hannah Arendt, "We Refugees," in *The Jewish Writings*

page 106: *"There is,"* as Plato said, *"thirst and no one drinks according to it."*

— R. J. Steward, *The Underworld Initiation*

page 106: *A sense that "underneath the concrete and underneath the towns an old ancient dreaming spirit is waiting for people to live in the right way, and when you do it you have a kind of genius underneath you that you as a person don't just possess."*

— Martin Shaw, "A Culture of Wildness" from *theschoolofmyth.com*. The blog seems to be no longer active.

ACKNOWLEDGEMENTS

Groundswell was supported by a research grant from the German Academic Exchange Service and an Arizona Commission on the Arts grant.

A version of "Augury" was published in the chapbook *Abraq ad Habra: I Will Create As I Speak* from Essay Press. Initial poems from "Pilgrimage" first appeared in *Tupelo Quarterly* and *Utterance*. "Oyneg Shabbes" appeared as part of "Groundvoices" in *Entropy*. "Prologue," "Grenze," "Hinterhaus" and "Formation" were featured by Tarpaulin Sky Press on their website. Poems based on "Notebook" were originally part of the manuscript *Embraces the carrion*.

I am indebted to many people I met along the way who offered their time, mind, and energy to my questions. Who went on walks and pilgrimages with me. Who hosted me and brought their own insights, doubts and critical reading to the work. Thank you, Lynn Friedland, Alexandra Appel, Nina Berfelde, Christian Hueck, Magda Abraham Diefenbach, Konstanze Jungbluth, Lothar Quinkenstein, Dominik Gerst, Antonina Balfanz, Werner Benecke, Karolina Stanek, Krzysztof Wojciechowski, Anastasia Rabin, Brandon Shimoda, Patrisia Gonzales, Josefina, Francisco Cantú,

Maegan Lopez, Robert Yerachmiel Sniderman, Mathias Svalina, John Pluecker, Ely Shipley, Poupeh Missaghi, Anna Fulford and Elizabeth J. Colen.

My gratitude to Annie Guthrie, whose generous and insightful feedback allowed me to complete the book at a moment when I had all but given up on it.

Thank you Uljana Wolf, Daniel Borzutzky and Jill Magi for your words.

And to everyone at Essay Press, deep appreciation for your care and dedicated labor.

Finally, I want to thank my Doolen Middle School students in Tucson with whom I wrote during the fall of 2016 upon my return from Germany, shivering together as we revealed our dreams and nightmares to the desert.

And to the many dead, named and unnamed, who cross these pages, their voices lifting briefly from the ground. I hope my listening and retelling has fed you.

YANARA FRIEDLAND is a writer and translator born in Berlin. Her first book *Uncountry: A Mythology* was the winner of the 2015 Noemi Press Fiction award and is published in German translation with Matthes & Seitz (2021). Her collection of essays *Groundswell* (Essay Press) has been supported by grants from the DAAD and Arizona Commission on the Arts. She currently lives in the Pacific Northwest, where she teaches at Fairhaven College of Interdisciplinary Studies and is writing a book on sleeplessness.

OTHER TITLES BY ESSAY PRESS

The Body: An Essay, Jenny Boully
Letters from Abu Ghraib, Joshua Casteel
A Prank of Georges, Thalia Field and Abigail Lang
Griffin, Albert Goldbarth
Adorno's Noise, Carla Harryman
I, Afterlife: Essay in Mourning Time, Kristen Prevallet
The Age of Virtual Reproduction, Spring Ulmer
Singing in Magnetic Hoofbeat, Will Alexander
this is the fugitive, misha pam dick
Ideal Suggestions: Essays in Divinatory Poetics, Selah Saterstrom
Of Sphere, Karla Kelsey
Litany for the Long Moment, Mary-Kim Arnold
Of Colour, Katherine Agyemaa Agard
Poem That Never Ends, Silvina López Medin